HONOR THY SOW BUG

BY DAVID SEABORG

*"Walk on the lighted path, always;
To yourself and the world, remain true."*

Beatitude PRESS
BERKELEY, CALIFORNIA

Printed in the United States of America
By Beatitude Press, Berkeley, California
Fourth Printing — April, 2010

ISBN: 978-0-9795651-2-0
Library of Congress Control Number: 2007907606

Front and Back Covers Designed by
David Seaborg and Doug Rees

Front Cover Art by Jillian Greenfelder
and Suzanne Kendall

Photograph on Back Cover:
David Seaborg in the backyard of his townhouse in California. He is holding his pet Desert Tortoise (*Gopherus agassizii*), which faces the threat of extinction and is protected. David has a permit to keep it legally, and adopted it when it was already captive and needed a home. The tortoise's name is Pedro. The orange, wooden horse with the author's last name in white letters is a Dalarna Horse, the well-known and loved folk art of the province of Dalarna, Sweden, where David's paternal grandmother came from. It is a gift from David's brother, Eric. David is in front of the garden of native plants that he planted to attract and feed several species of native bees, which are in danger of extinction because their natural food plants are being destroyed due to the paving over of their habitats. The plant behind David is a Bush Anemone (*Capenteria californica*). Native bees are good pollinators of many of our food crops. This photograph was taken by David's friend, Diddo Clark.

Feb. 24, 2012

To Wolfgang,

Thank you for your interest in my poetry and interesting intellect. I hope these poems inspire you. Best of luck in all you do,

David Seaborg

To my parents, Glenn and Helen Seaborg;
my siblings, Lynne Cobb, and Peter, Steve,
and Eric Seaborg; my nieces, Lela Arthur
and Molly Cobb; and my wife, Adele

i

*"A person could lose everything
in the flap of a duck's wing."*

TABLE OF CONTENTS

See the Alphabetized Index Of The Poems on page 241 for the page numbers of the Memorable Lines From The Poems and the Author's Commentary On The Poems, where the page number for both of these is listed for each individual poem.

EDITORIAL AND PERSONAL ACKNOWLEDGEMENTS

The following people gave helpful editorial advice and suggestions on the poems or other writings in this book. I will indicate whether the advice was of a specific or general nature where relevant, and briefly include any relevant information about each person who aided me. Gar Smith, the former editor of *Earth Island Journal*, the magazine of the environmental organization, Earth Island Institute, gave me the idea of having a picture of a man doing a namaste to a sow bug on cover of the book. My friend, Bill Ryan, gave editorial advice on the section called "The Reason For This Book's Title, And What Is A Sow Bug?". Robert Hass, who served two terms as U. S. Poet Laureate, and Lawrence Ferlinghetti, well-known poet, painter, and co-founder of City Lights Bookstore, in San Francisco, California, both gave helpful general editorial advice. I received good general and specific editorial suggestions from four teachers of four different poetry courses I took: Beth Houston, Richard Silberg, Cheryl Desmeril, and Leslie Kirk Campbell. Leslie Kirk Campbell also taught me effective ways of accessing my subconscious mind in her class, and this helped me in writing my poetry. In addition, she gave extensive specific editorial advice for several poems after the class was finished. A fellow student in Cheryl Desmeril's poetry class, Louise McGowan, gave excellent general and specific editorial advice on several poems. My friend, Peter DuMont, gave especially helpful specific editorial assistance on a number of poems, was very generous with his time, and was particularly helpful in making the longer version of "So Human a Predator" into a more effective and concise poem. Dr. Sterling Bunnell, poet, naturalist, and my good friend, listened to me read some of my poems to him, held interesting discussions with me about them, and acted as a source of inspiration and encouragement. Professional prose editor Walt Kleine tried his hand at the critique of poetry by giving a small amount of specific editorial advice on a few of the poems. My friend, Dennis Fritzinger, a poet, gave excellent general and specific editorial suggestions. Poet Rob Lipton gave some helpful general pointers. My sister, Lynne Cobb, gave invaluable, specific editorial advice on "Transcendence", and on how to best express the book's prose in a few specific areas.

My friend, poet, poetry critic, and Ph. D. in English from the University of California at Berkeley, Dr. Helene Knox, spent several hours reading many of the poems, writing specific and general feedback on them, and discussing them with me. Her editorial advice was invaluable.

I insist on scientific, historical, and any other relevant types of accuracy in my poetry, unless there is a good literary reason not to do so. Helene Knox helped ensure accuracy with respect to Biblical quotes of Jesus Christ in the poem, "Jesus, How you've Changed!". The following people advised me to ensure the scientific accuracy of some of the poems (most, but not all, advised on only one poem): Lepidopterist (one who studies butterflies and moths) Dr. Jerry Powell, and botanist Dr. Susan Jenkins, both faculty at the University of California at Berkeley; Dr. Frank Almeda, well-known botanist and Senior Curator of Botany at the California Academy of Sciences in San Francisco, California; Joe Willingham, newsletter editor and webmaster of the East Bay Chapter of the California Native Plant Society; Sue Rosenthal, Program Chair of the East Bay Chapter of the California Native Plant Society; Kerry Wilcox, Sanctuary Manager of the Richardson Bay Audubon Center and Sanctuary, in Tiburon, California; Shelby Starkey, an amateur ornithologist and volunteer with the Golden Gate Audubon Society; Chas Holt, Research Ecologist for the British Trust for Ornithology; my friend, Carl Trost, an amateur astronomer; and my friend, the aforementioned Dr. Sterling Bunnell.

I am ecstatic at the success of *Honor Thy Sow Bug*, for the first printing sold out. I made some improvements to the book for the second printing. I received valuable advice on these improvements from the following people: my siblings, Lynne Cobb, Steve Seaborg, and Eric Seaborg; my sister-in-law and Eric's wife, Ellen Dudley; my friends, Peter DuMont and poet H. D. Moe; and my friend and publisher at Beatitude Press, Doug Rees.

I thank all of the people listed above for their valuable input and advice, which I deeply, profoundly appreciate. The poems in this volume are better as a result of this editorial assistance and help on accuracy of the poems. Any areas in the poetry perceived by the reader as weaknesses are solely the fault of yours truly, the author, not those who aided me.

LITERARY ACKNOWLEDGEMENTS

My poem, "Sinner's Rue", was inspired by a poem of the same name, which is poem number XXX in the book called *Last Poems*, although my "Sinner's Rue" has a different theme than the poem that inspired it. My "In the Glen" was inspired by "Bredon Hill" (pronounced Breedon), which is poem number XXI in *A Shropshire Lad*; my "Springtime", by poem XXIII in *Last Poems*; and my "Nature's Nature", by poem XXVII in *Last Poems*. These four poems that served as inspiration to my poems are all by A. E. Housman, who gave titles to very few of his poems, labeling each of them with Roman numerals in the order that they appeared in each of his volumes of poetry, whether he named them or not. "Love Lies Still" was inspired by Lawrence Ferlinghetti's "Dove Sta Amore". "Highland Mary", by Robert Burns, inspired the rhythm for my "Succession". I conceived and was influenced in writing two poems, "Gaian Slumber" and "Black", as a result of an English translation of a poem originally written in Spanish by the Spanish poet, Federico Garcia Lorca, called "Somnabule Ballad", although both of these poems of mine have a very different subject and theme than Lorca's poem. I conceived the idea for my poem, "Duende", and ideas for some of its imagery and poetic language, from "Theory and Function of the Duende", a lecture delivered by Lorca, in Havana, Cuba, and Buenos Aires, Argentina, in the 1930's. It is published in *Lorca*, a book by this same Federico Garcia Lorca, translated from Spanish to English by J. L. Gili, published by Penguin Books, London, in 1960. "Silver", by Walter de la Mare, inspired and influenced my "Gold"; "All but Blind", by the same author, vaguely inspired my "Human and Mole". "Earth Drums" was inspired by "In a Station at the Metro", by Ezra Pound. To write "Reel Whiz Dumb", at the very least, I obtained ideas, and perhaps even borrowed some phrases, from traditions of wisdom from the Near to Far East, probably including some or all of the following traditions: Sufism, Buddhism, Hinduism, and Taoism. I did not do this consciously or intentionally. I am not aware of which phrases, if any, were borrowed; if all or only some of any given phrase was borrowed; or from where any phrases were borrowed. I took the title of "There's Nothing You Can Do that Can't Be Done" from a line in the Beatles' song, "All You Need Is Love". My poem, "So Human a Predator", has two versions, one much longer than the other. In the longer version of this poem only, I took the line "the forests of the night", from the same line in William Blake's poem, "The Tyger". However, these last two borrowings are obvious, purposeful poetic references to well-known works, acknowledged here only because of my compulsive need to avoid even the slightest hint of failing to credit those I borrow from. My poem, "Pieces of April", was inspired by a song by the rock and roll group, Three Dog Night, bearing the same name as this poem. Readers familiar with the poem, "The Second Coming", by William Butler Yeats, will recognize that I borrowed from a small part of this poem for part of the last stanza of my poem, "Jesus, How You've Changed!" In this case, Yeats was not an influence on my creating this poem's structure or theme; rather, I overtly and purposefully recalled the Yeats poem to the reader's mind for dramatic effect. "Neither Far out nor in Deep", by Robert Frost, provided inspiration for and influenced "Sky Wisdom". "I've Known Oceans" was inspired and influenced by "The Negro Speaks of Rivers", by Langston Hughes. For my poem, "No It U Love", I created some of the palindromes myself, but I borrowed the vast majority of them from known existing ones. To write my poem, "The Origin of Species", I took the last paragraph of Charles Darwin's master work that presents his theory of evolution by natural selection, the book entitled *The Origin of Species* (published in 1859). I added my own line breaks, changed some of the wording and punctuation a small amount, and changed some capitalized words to lower case, to make it into a poem. My sister, Lynne Cobb, did the same exercise of writing a poem based on this magnificent paragraph and showed it to me before I wrote this poem. Hence, I adopted her idea, and she deserves credit for the concept of my poem. I conceived the idea for "Poem Without End" from a song I saw on the television show, "Sesame Street"; the concept for this poem is not original, and has appeared in a few songs and other works in our culture. I was also influenced in the writing of a few other poems in this book, though less than in the cases listed above and in too general a way to mention any specific poems, by Jelaluddin Rumi and Wallace Stevens. The works of Rumi that influenced my poetry were English translations from Persian (Farsi), the original language that he wrote them in. Except for "The Origin of Species" poem, I did not borrow enough from the aforementioned authors—or, to put it more positively, I was sufficiently original—that giving any of them co-authorship is not merited.

ABOUT THE AUTHOR

David Seaborg is an evolutionary biologist who does scientific research on evolutionary theory. He has a Bachelor of Science degree from the University of California at Davis, and a Master of Arts degree from the University of California at Berkeley, both in zoology. He originated an important theory that states that organisms can act as feedback systems with respect to their evolution, and that their morphology and behavior play approximately as large a role as their environment in shaping their evolution. In this theory, occasionally traits of organisms become involved in positive feedback loops, leading to very rapid evolutionary change. Also, this idea is a possible mechanism for the important idea of punctuated equilibrium, proposed by Niles Eldredge and Stephen Jay Gould. He has taught biology at all levels. David Seaborg is a distinguished, active environmental leader, who founded and heads the World Rainforest Fund, a nonprofit foundation dedicated to saving the earth's tropical rainforests and biodiversity. He also founded and heads the Glenn T. Seaborg Greater Lafayette Open Space Fund, a nonprofit foundation named after his father and dedicated to preserving open space in the greater Lafayette, California, area. He wrote an article that is a summary of the scientific research on the effects of high atmospheric levels of carbon dioxide other than global warming. Unlike the climatic effects, these effects are not well known to the general public. They are very serious, and have the potential to cause high levels of extinction of species and greatly disrupt ecosystems and our food supply. David carried the Ten Commandments for the Earth, a version of the original Ten Commandments re-written to focus on saving the earth's environment, while riding a camel down Mount Sinai, allegedly the mountain in Egypt down which Moses carried the original Ten Commandments. Then, in a brief ceremony, he presented these Ten Commandments to a Bedouin youth, who represented the indigenous people and the youth of the planet, the generation inheriting the earth for its stewardship. After completing this act, which was captured on video camera, David swam for over an hour with a wild dolphin in the Red Sea. David conceived the idea for and was a leading organizer for a press conference of Nobel Prize winners on global environmental issues and world poverty that was held at the time of the 100th Nobel Prize ceremony in Stockholm, Sweden, in December, 2001. He was elected at the Democratic Party caucus as an alternate delegate to the Democratic National Convention in Denver, Colorado, in August, 2008, where he got three planks added to the Democratic Party platform: conservation and development of alternative energy to reduce global warming, saving biodiversity, and reducing nuclear weapons by verifiable treaty. He was one of three winners in the 2008 Golden Gate National Recreation Area Big Year competition, a project with over 200 participants to save and observe the thirty-three threatened and endangered species that occur in this national recreation area. David has been to over 30 countries, observing various natural ecosystems and wildlife. He is an award-winning nature and wildlife photographer, and an award-winning poet. He is listed is in *Who's Who In America*. An excellent public speaker, he lectures to various scientific, environmental, civic, business, and other organizations on evolutionary biology, the philosophical implications of science, and environmental issues.

He has had a number of his poems published by The National Library of Poetry (Owings Mills, Maryland), in anthologies of collected poetry by several different poets. These poems, and the anthologies they appeared in, are: "Nature's Nature", in *At Water's Edge* (1995); "Green to Green", in *Tranquil Rains of Summer* (1998), and again in *America at the Millenium* (1999); "Siddhartha Gautama", in *From the Mountaintop* (2000); "Midnight", in *Immortal Verses* (2006); and "Springtime", in *The International Who's Who of Poetry* (2007).* His "Once upon a Cloudless Sulphur" was the poem of the week of the Butterfly Gardener's Association during one week in February, 2007.

---

* With the probable exception of "Springtime" and possible exception of "Midnight", the versions of these poems published in these volumes are somewhat different than the ones published in this book, since the author made some improvements on these poems since their publication by the National Library of Poetry.

xiv

THE REASON FOR THIS BOOK'S TITLE, AND WHAT IS A SOW BUG?

This book of poetry is entitled *Honor Thy Sow Bug*. This volume contains no poems that are about or even mention sow bugs. Its name encompasses and refers to the poetry in a subtle, abstract, whimsical, and poetic manner. The book's title is intuitive and right-brained. It also has humor in it. I arrived at the title when I first started writing the volume, purely by intuition, a message from my subconscious mind that I did not make any effort to attain. Once the idea hit me, no doubt more from my right cerebral hemisphere than my left, I loved the title, decided to stick with it, and never wavered from this decision.

It was not until years after I thought of the title that I thought of the following reasons why it is so appropriate for this book. *Honor Thy Sow Bug* has poems on environmental issues that favor saving our earth and its species, and some sow bug species are recyclers, being detritus eaters. The book has poems on nature, and sow bugs are very much a part of nature and can be construed as symbolic of it. It has poems on spiritual issues, and it is certainly spiritual to honor something smaller than ourselves and that can symbolize nature, both of which are true of sow bugs. There are poems on death, and many sow bug species eat dead organisms. This book has some humorous poems and some poems with humor in them, and the title is humorous. Of course, there are poems about topics in this volume that the title does not refer to, such as those about romantic love. But few if any possible titles for this volume could make reference to all eighty of its poems, and at any rate this is not an issue.

Some readers may wonder: What is a sow bug? They are small, gray animals of the genus *Porcellio* that look like, but are not, insects, and often live in people's gardens. The sow bug resembles the pill bug, which rolls into a ball when threatened, and is often called a roly-poly. But sow bugs are different animals than pill bugs, and cannot roll into balls, relying instead on an awful taste to deter predators. There are many species of sow bugs. Sow bugs are not sows because sows are female pigs, and sow bugs are not pigs and only half of them are female (about). They are not bugs either. To the layman, bugs are insects, and sow bugs are not insects. To the scientist, bugs are a specific type of insect. But if sow bugs are not insects, they can't be a specific type of insect. (Say you are trying to figure out if you are an almond. Say you are not any kind of a nut. You are probably some kind of nut if you are sitting around trying to figure out if you're an almond, but let's say you are not a nut at all. Then you can't be an almond, because that's a kind of nut.) They are a kind of arthropod; more specifically, they are isopods, which are crustaceans, which include crabs and shrimp. Do sow bugs taste like shrimp? I don't know. I have never eaten shrimp.

Isopod means equal leg, so in theory their seven pairs of legs are of equal length, but the male needs sex. So the first two appendages on the male abdomen are modified as elongated organs for copulation. Leaf-like growths called brood pouches on the underside of females at the base of some legs hold developing eggs (up to a hundred) and embryos. But the juveniles, which resemble adults, are liberated (though they hardly would view it as such) from the pouch at an early age, and sow bugs have nothing in common with marsupials other than this pouch. If you confuse a sow bug with a kangaroo, the results of your I. Q. test will be negative. And you would probably stay up all night studying for your urine test.

They live in dark, moist places, often under things like rocks, boards, and leaf litter. They breathe with gills, so they are restricted to moist places. People don't breathe with gills, so none are restricted to moist places. I wish some people were. Then I would go to a dry place. Some species are nocturnal. All the nocturnal species are active at night. They shun light; I'm not so sure if they shun redundancy. Sow bugs eat dead and decaying plants, turning them into compost, being great recyclers and improvers of the soil. They will also eat live plants.

They provide food for birds, lizards, other vertebrates, and some invertebrates. They do not do this intentionally. They do not act as waiters, waitresses, or food servers. They do it by getting eaten. I added those last three sentences to avoid ambiguity (give me ambiguity or give me something else). They have in fact evolved adaptations to avoid being eaten. For example, some species roll up into a ball to protect themselves when disturbed, putting their head in proximity to the area where they pass their waste. I have heard some people being accused of a similar anatomy without having to bother to roll into a ball. (Maybe our gene pool could use a little chlorine).

They have a skeleton on their exterior that they shed (molt) periodically, in two stages. First, the back half molts; then, two or three days later, the front half molts. The previous sentence is not a joke. Really.

They have a pair of appendages at the rear of the body called uropods. What are the uropods for? I don't know. Ask a sow bug expert. Don't ask a sow bug. They do not talk, certainly not to a human asking them what they do with their uropods. Uropod. Sounds like someone is calling you what pea plants hold their peas in.

In captivity, they need a moist towel in their container or they will die. That's right, they can be kept as pets, and don't bite, don't bite them.

INTRODUCTION

I hope this volume, my first book of poetry, presents an alternative to American poetry of today. I claim that poetry in America today belongs to a subculture that is not part of the literary mainstream; that it is largely invisible, irrelevant, and ignored by the general reader, who does not like it, but does, as a whole, like the poetry of times previous to it; that it is practiced by a small group isolated from the mainstream; that it lacks, in large part, artistic competence; and that poetry used to be cherished, enjoyed, and held in high regard by the general reader. Let me present some evidence for this thesis.

In 1988, Joseph Epstein wrote the critique, "Who Killed Poetry?" This essay first appeared in *Commentary*, then was reprinted in *AWP Chronicle*, the journal of the Associated Writing Programs. In this essay, Epstein contrasted the Modernists, the generation including Wallace Stevens (1879-1955) and T. S. Elliot (1888-1965), with contemporary poets who followed them. He argued that the Modernists were artists with a broad cultural vision who accomplished major achievements, while contemporary poets operated within the isolated world of the university as "poetry professionals", bearing the fruit of only minor accomplishments at best. Epstein claimed the poets themselves and the institutions they had helped bring into being, especially creative-writing programs, were at fault for what he saw as a sorry plight of poetry.

Well-known poet and literary essayist Dana Gioia wrote an interesting article published in *The Atlantic Monthly*, in May, 1991, entitled, "Can Poetry Matter?" This article became the title essay of his book, *Can Poetry Matter?* (Graywolf, 1992). In this influential essay, he argues that contemporary American poetry has become irrelevant to the general reader of today. He says it currently belongs to a subculture. He contends that it is no longer part of our artistic and intellectual mainstream; is the specialized work of a relatively small, isolated group; and little of its fruit receives notice outside that closed group.

Gioia makes the point that this happens, surprisingly, at a time when poetry is undergoing unprecedented expansion. There has never before been so much poetry published: so many new books of poetry, poetry anthologies, and poetry journals. Close to a thousand new poetry collections are published each year, along with a huge amount of verse printed in various magazines. It has never been so easy to earn a living as a poet; there are several thousand college-level jobs in teaching creative writing. Congress and twenty-five states have positions of poet laureate. Public support in the form of federal, state, and local agencies is abundant; and private fellowships, prizes, and subsidized retreats abound. And there has never been so much published criticism of the art (although, as I will discuss, this criticism is hardly honest and does not tend to attack contemporary poetry when it is called for). All of this is spectacular by any historical measure.

Gioia points out that the problem is that the poetry boom is disturbingly confined. A professional elite created by decades of public and private funding churns out and reads new poetry. This class of people is composed of teachers, graduate students, editors, publishers, and administrators. They have become the almost exclusive audience for contemporary poetry. They are based mainly in universities. As a result of this situation, American verse, once directed outward, is now more and more directed inward. Contemporary poetry is read by other poets, and essentially no one else.

Since readers see so much low-quality poetry published and even praised, most readers of today assume that no significant new poetry is being written or published. General readers constitute the audience that poetry once had, but has now lost. Gioia calls this loss of general readership the final isolation of poetry as an art form in contemporary society.

He cites evidence to support his argument by pointing out that daily newspapers once reviewed poetry, but no longer do, although they review other forms of literature. More than this, there is scant coverage of poetry or even poets in the general press. The National Book Awards dropped poetry as a category from 1984 onward. Leading critics almost never review verse; in fact, almost nobody except other poets review it. Virtually no collections of contemporary poetry are published except those exclusively targeting an academic audience, not a popular one. It appears that the large number of readers that still enjoy good fiction hardly notice poetry. A reader familiar with the leading contemporary fiction authors would likely not recognize the names of today's leading poets.

Further evidence of the irrelevance of today's verse to the general reader comes from the response to Gioia's article. He received a tremendously positive reaction, far beyond what he or his editors anticipated. He received letters in thick bundles for months, with a total of over 400 letters from *Atlantic* readers. They were overwhelmingly favorable, with many stating he did not go far enough in criticizing contemporary poetry's isolation. Reporters phoned him for interviews; numerous newspaper and magazine articles about his essay appeared; radio producers asked him for on-the-air discussions of the article; friends phoned him with anecdotes about the article's impact; strangers phoned for advice. He heard from countless people who care passionately for poetry, and was surprised by the emotion of their letters. They felt alienated from the self-enclosed world of today's verse, and were angry at the university for sequestering it. He was also shocked at how many readers resent modernism–which they also associate with the university–for killing the traditional forms of verse they love. Furthermore, there was a tone of hopeless resignation in many of the letters. They confided to him that Americans had stopped reading poetry, and little could be done to alleviate the situation. He also received newspaper clippings from friends showing that readers and writers across the United States were vigorously debating the issues he had raised. It is clear that general readers of poetry are disenfranchised. He writes about the response to his article in a short piece called "Hearing from Poetry's Audience", printed in *Poetry Review* (U.K.), spring, 1992.

Further evidence for the thesis that Americans do not appreciate contemporary verse and find it irrelevant can be found in the results of a survey conducted by the National Opinion Research Center at the University of Chicago and commissioned by the Poetry Foundation. It was based on 1,023 interviews conducted over a four-month period beginning in June, 2005. This was a random sample of American adults who read newspapers, magazines, and books for pleasure, and who read primarily in English. Both current and former readers of poetry were asked to name their favorite poems. Essentially all of the poems at the top of the list were the older classics of poetry that used formal rhyme and meter. For example, Edgar Allen Poe's "The Raven" topped the list, and high on the list were Robert Frost's "Stopping by Woods on a Snowy Evening" and "The Road not Taken". This not only shows the irrelevance of contemporary verse to the American reader, it shows an appreciation and love of the poetry of past eras, and of formal rhyme and meter.

Furthermore, Gioia is not alone in his view among scholars who have written on the subject of today's verse. John McWhorter expresses a similar, though not identical, view to Gioia's, in his book, *Doing Our Own Thing*, subtitled, *The Degradation of Language and Music and Why We Should, Like, Care*, published by Gotham Books (New York, 2003), and at least one other publisher. Although the main theme of the book is what McWhorter considers to be the degradation of language in general, he discusses poetry. He argues that Americans do not cherish poetry, the way people all over the rest of the world do. He goes on to assert that our poets just talk, and no longer write in heightened language that follows strict rules of structure and rhyme. He clearly disapproves of this.

It is certainly not true that poetry never mattered to the general reading audience in America. In fact, this self-enclosed condition of today's poetry is unprecedented, and a recent phenomenon. Before this fall of poetry, it was enjoyed and cherished by the general public. Henry Wadsworth Longfellow achieved international fame. His "The Courtship of Miles Standish" sold 15,000 copies on its first day of publication. John Greenleaf Whittier helped inspire the Abolitionist movement through his poetry, and had a town named after him. His poems were not only memorized, but set to music as hymns. The first volumes of Emily Dickinson's poetry were very popular with the general public, mostly in New England, when they were first published in the 1890's. James Whitcomb Riley's birthday became a state holiday in Indiana. President Woodrow Wilson inquired anxiously about Riley's condition during his final illness. A. E. Housman's first book of poems, *A Shropshire Lad* (1896), sold slowly at first, but then struck a chord with British and American readers and became popular, and a lasting success. Several musical composers found inspiration in his poetry. President Theodore Roosevelt reviewed the poetry of Edward Arlington Robinson, whose later books attained the best-seller list. Edna St. Vincent Millay had such a large following that she was hired to deliver a series of poetry readings on commercial radio. Robert Frost spoke at President Kennedy's 1961 inauguration, reciting his poem, "The Gift Outright", written in 1942. He achieved worldwide fame, as millions of readers around the globe found comfort and profound meaning in his poetry. In addition to influencing other poets, Frost influenced numerous authors of other genres, musicians, and playwrights into the 21st century. Carl Sandburg was invited to address a joint session of Congress. The Welsh poet, Dylan Thomas, was a sensation when he gave readings in America in 1949 and the early 1950's. E. E. Cummings was very popular among the general public in the 1960's. I could cite scores of other examples.

I have read contemporary poetry, and heard it at readings and spoken word events. Having presented what I consider to be strong evidence for contemporary poetry's isolation and irrelevance, let me give my own impressions from my experience of it. I find that it tends to be self-important, snobbish, and cliquish. It is as if there is a set of rules or accepted ways of writing that must be followed, and those who do not follow these rules are not considered "cool", are not accepted as a member of the club. To be acceptable to the judgmental Inquisitors of the art, one must not have meter or rhyme. In fact, a prosaic feel, style, and form are preferable to any rhythm or rhyme. The subject should be something rather trivial and lacking in relevance to the general reader. The universal ideas and feelings that move us and have appeared in poetry through the ages, such as nature, romantic love, and death, seem to be considered unsophisticated and not cool. It is much better to write about the angst caused by your roommate's messy toothbrush. Skill is not a valued quality, or, if it is, it is at any rate sorely lacking. There is an attempt at imagery and originality, although it often falls short. At least these latter two are valued. One gets the impression that these writers do not understand the art of poetry. It seems as if little effort or thought went into writing many of the poems, that they were produced quickly. Sometimes they are political; in these cases, they drip with a political correctness that goes very well with their self-righteous quality. It is the preachy, holier-than-thou attitude of poetry written according to the strict rules of the elite club that is to me the most irritating aspect of much contemporary poetry, especially since most of it is not very good or skillful. Also, it is very boring, failing to hold my interest. I feel I would rather be doing something else when I read contemporary poetry, and that it is hard to finish a poem because it does not hold my attention. Finally, it is often incomprehensible, not because of an elegant ambiguity that can enhance a poem; rather, incomprehensibility is a treasured quality in and of itself that helps with acceptance to the elite club. This brings to mind Woody Allen's joke in one of his books that a certain writer, philosopher, or artist (I do not recall which) was the most incomprehensible, hence the best, of his genre. Additionally, reading contemporary poems often gives me the feeling that they are difficult to comprehend due to the author's lack of skill. All of these weaknesses together result in an effect reminiscent of the story of the emperor with no clothes, and the impression that there is an attempt, conscious or not, to con the reader into thinking that he or she is missing the profound greatness and skill due to lack of the reader's ability to appreciate it, when in fact there is nothing there to appreciate. The elitist feeling that many of today's poets convey of belonging to an exclusive club that readers are not part of leaves one with the feeling that their readers are expected to appreciate their writing or be looked at as uneducated philistines.

The bias against rhyme and rhythmic meter is so great that a school of poetry called New Formalism, which advocates that poetry have rhyme and meter, has been born in reaction to it. Advocates of a formal style with rules different from those of most contemporary poetry, rhyme, and rhythm lament the abandonment of the beauty of rhyme and meter, which they consider a major defining strength of poetry and source of its artistic and pleasing qualities, and protest against what they see as a lack of attention to poetic language and its replacement with prosaic wording.

Some people disagree, objecting to the tendency in poetry with rhyme and rhythm to fall into simple, unoriginal, greeting card verse, with predictable, monotonous, rocking-horse rhythms. They object to simple rhymes with commonly-used rhyme words that they consider to be clichés, such as rhyming "moon" with "June". They also caution that the need for rhythm and rhyme can govern the structure of the poem. For example, it can force the use of words for the sole purpose of maintaining the rhythm. Too much attention to rhyme and meter can result in the lack of vivid imagery or other poetic strengths. Of course, this is all true in unskilled poetry with rhythm and rhyme, but not the skilled verse of this nature. I bring this up to point out that both views are partly right and partly wrong, for it is not the presence or absence of rhyme and meter that determine the quality of a poem, but the skill that the poet displays in writing rhymed and metered poetry or free verse. Both can be excellent or bad poetry, depending on the poet's skill and ability to avoid the pitfalls that each side warns against. The subject, message, and method by which the poet wants to convey the poem's message should determine which of these alternatives the poet chooses to use, and even the finer details of the poem's form and style. I think that the form of a poem should be consistent with its subject. Therefore, a good poet should be skilled at a variety of forms of poetry. I think today's verse frequently misses these points badly, often writing poetry that is too prosaic, frequently slacking on the attention, time, and effort required to create a skilled piece of work. Also, the contemporary poet often chooses to write in free verse because it is the accepted "club" convention, without considering whether the poem's subject and message could more effectively be achieved by a more formal style. I must point out that poetic forms are not best classified as simply free verse and formal rhymed and metered verse. There are many intermediate forms that have aspects of both, so classification of poetic forms is far more complex than a grouping into two classes. Discussions about which poetic form is best have often reflected this complexity, and were not necessarily merely debates between the merits of free verse as opposed to verse with rhyme and rhythm. And discussions concerning which poetic forms are the best ones are not new; they have been going on at least since Walt Whitman's first free verse.

The reasons for the deterioration and lack of relevance of today's poetry are worth discussing briefly. The first reason that I see is also another criticism I have of contemporary poetry: It lacks the self-corrective function provided by criticism, including self-criticism. In fact, it is likely that part of the reason that so much poor poetry is published today is that the hard work of evaluation and criticism have been largely abandoned. To the extent that there is outside criticism, it is largely ignored. The poet Robert Bly, in his book, *American Poetry: Wildness and Domesticity* (Harper and Row, New York, 1990), wrote: "We have an odd situation: although more bad poetry is being published now than ever before in American history, most of the reviews are positive...the country is full of young poets and readers who are confused by seeing mediocre poetry praised, or never attacked, and who end up doubting their own critical perceptions." Gioia says that the general press has largely abandoned evaluation, and the press specializing in the criticism of poetry has grown so protective of it that it disdains making unflattering judgments. I think that without self-criticism and attention to honest outside criticism, any endeavor will tend to deteriorate. It must be stressed that reviewers of today have their primary loyalty to their poets and publishers, while reviewers of fifty years ago had their primary loyalty to the readers. Another reason for the irrelevance of contemporary verse, which I mentioned earlier, is the decades of funding that helped create the professional elite of poetry writers that became isolated, mainly in the university. Another reason, at least according to Gioia, is that poetry anthologies tend not to be compiled for readers outside the university. Editors have found that the best way to get an anthology assigned as reading for poetry courses is to include work by poets who teach the courses. Gioia says that many of these anthologies give the impression that literary quality is a concept that neither an editor nor a reader should take too seriously. Another important cause of the problem is that, for purposes of job security and career advancement, professional poets must publish, just as in other academic departments. "Publish or perish" is a well known adage in science, and the same holds true for the university poet. The more such a poet publishes, the faster the career progression. Therefore, quality suffers for the sake of quantity. Yet another reason that the poetry of today is ignored by the general population is the proliferation of competing media and activities, such as television, movies, and the Internet. A decline in humanities education and education in general in America, at all levels from kindergarten through the twelfth grade, and in some cases through college, is also a factor. A final reason is the unfortunate decline of literacy and increase in the number of non-readers in America. Indeed, recent statistics show that Americans are reading far less of everything, not just poetry, than in the past. They are reading less fiction and science. They are replacing reading with computer games, television, spectator sports, and other forms of mass entertainment.

The last three related and over-lapping reasons for the decline in interest in contemporary poetry of the general reader are not the fault of today's verse, and show that there are other reasons than the self-imposed isolation and decline in quality of today's poetry for its being ignored. However, I hold that the evidence and arguments listed earlier in this introduction clearly show that a significant portion of this problem, and certainly an unacceptably large part of it, is the fault of poetry's elite, self-induced isolation and self-inflicted irrelevance, and the production of shoddy work.

Let me make it clear that I do not think that all contemporary poetry is guilty of the charges I have listed, nor is it all unskillfully written. There are good contemporary poets. Examples include Adrienne Rich, Donald Justice, Mary Oliver, W. S. Merwin, William Stafford, and several others. The problem is that there is so much bad poetry published that the good is buried, and people assume nothing of note is being published.

Also, Dana Gioia wrote an essay called *Disappearing Ink: Poetry at the End of Print Culture*, in a book that is another collection of his essays. The book has the same name as the *Disappearing Ink* essay, and is published by Graywolf Press (Saint Paul, Minnesota, 2004). In this essay, Gioia defines popular poetry as the new forms of verse that have emerged outside the official literary culture, and which include such things as rap, cowboy poetry, and spoken word poetry with its poetry slams. He contrasts this with literary poetry, which he defines as all written, high-art poetry of all types and schools. He argues, and I agree, that popular poetry does have a large following. However, he does not necessarily consider popular poetry good poetry as a whole. I also do not think it is necessarily generally very good. It is oral and not printed, being performed in front of audiences. The arguments presented in this introduction are not concerned with popular poetry, since the poems in *Honor Thy Sow Bug* are literary poetry, and my remarks are about the quality and relevance to the general reader of this latter genre. I include this paragraph solely for the sake of completeness, and encourage the interested reader to read Gioia's essay.

I acknowledge that my case would be strengthened, or at least more easily evaluated, with examples of contemporary poetry that would allow the reader to judge the merits of my harsh criticisms of it. However, the tremendous volume of such verse insures that it would be impossible to present a statistically significant and convincingly unbiased sample in an essay of this length. I encourage the reader who has not already done so and who wants more data to evaluate my criticisms to read poems from anthologies or magazines of contemporary poetry. A good series of such anthologies is *The Best American Poetry* series, which is published annually, and offers a selection of poems published over the course of a year, chosen by a different distinguished poet who acts as guest editor each year. The series editor is David Lehman. The publisher is Scribner Poetry (New York, New York). The title of each book is *The Best American Poetry*, followed by the year of publication. It is still being published; the last volume to come out at this writing is 2007. Guest editors really are distinguished poets; they have included Adrienne Rich, Robert Bly, and Robert Hass. Thus, the series provides a broad sampling of the best truly contemporary poetry, a fair sample from which to evaluate my criticisms.

Since I have been so critical of today's poetry, I have some obligation to answer the question: What do I think constitutes a good to great, skillfully written poem? Let me briefly list the qualities of a such a poem. This is not intended to be a comprehensive list. Among other reasons, it is presented to give the reader, especially the less experienced in the art of reading and enjoying poetry, a basis for evaluation of the points in this essay, contemporary poetry, poetry in general, and my poetry in this book. And poets can use it to evaluate and improve their own poetry. It is also meant to stimulate thought. Not every quality I list below need be present for a poem to be good; there could be excellent poems that lack some of these criteria.

First, as I have stated earlier in this introduction, good poetry has what I call unity of subject/theme/goal and form/style. What the poem is about and what its author wants to convey and evoke in the reader should be consistent with and supported by the rhyme scheme or lack thereof, rhythm, line breaks, and other relevant poetic devices. For example, if the poem is talking about a dead person or something that does not move, words of only one syllable can re-enforce this, sometimes with great emotional effect. To give a simple example that makes my point clear, Robert Frost's poem, "Nothing Gold Can Stay", talks about how beautiful things do not last, and is itself a short poem. I point out several examples of unity of subject and form in the poems in this volume in the section called "Author's Commentary On The Poems", a section that I will describe later in this introduction.

Second, a characteristic of good poetry is multidimensionality. Good poems tend to say more than meets the eye and what is on the surface, making statements that are not stated overtly, but can be deduced from the text. Much of the meaning is between the lines. The good poem may have more than one interpretation. It often has more than one layer of meaning. These layers often reinforce each other, but may contradict each other. This may be done by the use of symbolism, irony, or any other poetic device.

Third, a good poem has beautiful, delightful language. It sounds wonderful. This may or may not be achieved by rhyme and rhythm. Generally, even in free verse, a pleasing rhythm, even if subtle, is something I like. And I love a nice rhythm in formal verse. Sound of the poem is a key feature in its beauty and conveying its message. As a result, to the poet, there are no such things as true synonyms, because the sound of a word is a fundamental part of its essence and, in a poem, sound can affect a word's or phrase's meaning. Because of this, poetry can never be adequately translated from another language, because translation, no matter how skillfully done, cannot bring the sounds of the original language with it. This does not mean one should never read poetry originally written in and translated from a foreign tongue, because to do so would cause the reader to miss some beautiful work that can be enjoyed in spite of the inherent problem discussed here. However, one should be aware of this problem when reading poetry translated from another language.

Fourth, a good poem should have echoic properties. These are delightful, and are one way that poetry is distinguished from prose. These include end and internal rhymes, near rhymes of various forms, rhythm, alliteration, assonance, references to earlier lines, and other such techniques.

Fifth, a poem should move its reader emotionally. A good measure of a poem's success is how deeply it touches us. An effective poet does not express himself or herself; he or she expresses all of ourselves.

Sixth, good poetry is original in its use of language, sometimes even breaking entirely new ground. The language is fresh, and avoids clichés.

Seventh, a poem should have right-brained language, intuitive wording from the creative part of the brain; for example, phrases and ideas that typically appear in dreams.

Eighth, I think poems should be scientifically and historically accurate, and accurate in any other relevant factual way, unless there is a compelling literary, poetic reason that overrides this. That is to say, a poem should not speak of wild zebras living in Australia. Of course, there are obvious exceptions to this rule, in some cases when the poet is speaking metaphorically or otherwise not literally.

Ninth, a good poem has a unity of theme. It does not have any words that are irrelevant to or do not add to its overall effect, goal, or theme. It does not jump around to points or thoughts that have nothing to do with the rest of the poem, but sticks to its theme. It is focused.

Finally, a poem should be easily comprehensible and understandable, unless there a good reason for it not to be. This rule of comprehensibility has exceptions. Sometimes multiple meanings or glorious, delightful ambiguity can be used by the poet to great effect. Sometimes writing a work that allows for multiple interpretations that are more or less equally valid is very delightfully moving. Sometimes it is effective to force the reader to think, not spelling out the meaning of the verse; this can make for a great work of poetry, and a meditation for the reader to grow spiritually, psychologically, inwardly. And often the use of right-brain, dream-like, intuitive language should not be sacrificed for clarity, especially if such a sacrifice causes the poet to over-explain some or all of the poem. This means a fine line often has to be drawn between comprehensibility and the various factors discussed here that call for ambiguity. However, comprehensibility should never be sacrificed because of lack of skill of the poet, or the poet's need to impress readers or fellow poets. I have cited this point of lack of comprehensibility above as one of my objections to today's poetry. I hope that the poems I present to you in this book have found the line between comprehensibility and the reasons counter to it discussed here, and that they are not unnecessarily incomprehensible.

My idea of what qualities constitute a good poem may be further illustrated by mentioning some of the poets I love. My favorite poets include A. E. Housman, Robert Frost, Edgar Allan Poe, William Shakespeare, Edwin Arlington Robinson, Robert Burns, Alfred Noyes, Edna St. Vincent Millay, Walter de la Mare, William Blake, Thomas Gray, Samuel Taylor Coleridge, Percy Bysshe Shelley, Gerard Manley Hopkins, Dylan Thomas, E. E. Cummings, Jalal ad-Din Rumi, Bob Dylan, Phil Ochs, William Wordsworth, Sir Walter Raleigh, Robert Herrick, John Masefield, Rudyard Kipling, Langston Hughes, and Alfred, Lord Tennyson. My two favorite poems are "The Rhyme of the Ancient Mariner", by Coleridge, and "The Raven", by Poe. Recall my caution concerning the difficulty of translating poetry from other languages. I have tremendous respect for Rumi, since he became a favorite poet of mine, in spite of the fact that his poems as I read them were translated into English, since he wrote in Persian (Farsi), a language I do not speak. Federico Garcia Lorca deserves a similar tribute, since he influenced three of my poems, two with a poem of his, one with an essay. I read translated versions of both of these works of his, for he wrote in Spanish, which I speak only a few words of.

I think that much of contemporary poetry falls short because it tends to lack the qualities that I think make high quality verse that I listed above. I hope this book serves as an alternative to the irrelevance and lack of life, and ability to move and touch us, of today's verse. I cannot claim that I have succeeded; only that I tried my best. I do know that I feel a sense of pleasure and delight in reading the poems in this book, and I have always believed if one can please oneself with one's work, one will tend to please others. Much to my delight, of the handful of friends and colleagues that I have shown several of the poems in this volume to, as a whole, they said that they thought the poetry was excellent, and that they enjoyed it. This includes poets, poetry teachers, Ph.D.'s in English and related fields, and professional poetry critics. It also includes friends and family, many of whom have no great experience as interpreters, much less writers or critics, of poetry. I hope and think this collection of my poetry does provide an alternative to the deficiencies of today's poetry. However, I did not write this volume solely for that purpose, although it is one important goal of the book. Another is my desire for this book to bring about a start in, and make a significant contribution toward, re-capturing the lost audience of poetry, re-awakening an interest in poetry in today's general public. May this work start a renaissance, a revolution, of interest in the average American in the art of reading, interpreting, and, above all, enjoying and taking deep pleasure from, that beautiful craft called poetry. Another goal and hope is that it will have an impact and influence on contemporary poetry, influencing other poets of today to write poetry that is exciting, moving, pleasurable, and relevant to the general public. Other goals of *Honor Thy Sow Bug* were for me to have fun and enjoy the pleasure of writing poetry, awaken my creativity in writing good verse, write excellent poetry for its own sake, give pleasure and enjoyment to the reader, and to awaken the inner being of the reader. Another way of saying the last objective, to clarify it, is to raise the consciousness of, or ignite spiritual and/or psychological growth in, the reader.

In some of the poems, new stanzas start at the beginning of a page, so it is not possible to put a space between stanzas to indicate a new stanza is starting. Often in these cases, one can tell a new stanza is beginning because all stanzas have the same number of lines and basic form. The problem occurs in the poem, "I Dream of Ebony", but here all stanza breaks are obvious, because every stanza ends with the same four-word refrain in four stair-step lines, thusly: "I

       dream

    of

      ebony."

In the poems where there is no cue to designate that a new stanza is beginning, I opted not to indicate it by a symbol at the top of the page, since this would look strange, and distract the reader from the poem. One can use one's judgment to determine the location of these new stanzas. However, for those who want to be sure, here is a list of the fourteen poems with invisible stanza breaks, and the pages that start with the new, invisible stanza at their top: "Eyes of Chocolate", pages 12 and 13; "Never Cry", pages 26 and 27; "Metamorphosis", page 39; "Transcendence", pages 41 and (obviously at this point in the poem) 42; "Reel Whiz Dumb", page 55; "The Sky Was Silent and the Moon Was White", page 62; "The Magpie", pages 68 and 69; "So Human a Predator" (longer version), pages 74 and 75; "Winds of August", pages 88 and 89; "No It U Love", pages 94 and 95; "Fingers of Nightshade", page 102; ""Duende", page 106; "Marriage in the Key of Ebony and Ivory", pages 108 and 109; "Jesus, How You've Changed!", page 118.

I have put the poems in order by topic, according to my best judgment, as best I could. Surely, there are other ways to order them than by subject matter, and many different possible orders the poems could be put in using this criterion. However, I am happy enough with my result.

Following the poems is a section entitled "Author's Commentary On The Poems". Here, I give helpful explanations and comments about the poem being discussed as a whole, or a specific part or parts of it. This section is for novices at reading, interpreting, and enjoying poetry; those who wish to explore the poems more deeply; those who are thorough and want to ensure they do not miss any major aspects of the poems; and those who simply might be interested. It is also intended to stimulate thought about the poems. This section does not translate or explain the meaning of the poems; this would a silly, bad idea. This is because poetry cannot be adequately translated into more understandable language or explained, for it derives much of its meaning and power not only from the meaning of its words, but the sound of the words, line breaks, and so on. Poetry is a compression, deriving much of its power from being concise. Explanations are decompressions that rob this power. Carl Sandburg, the Swedish American poet, was once asked to explain the meaning of one of his poems. He asked the questioner, to paraphrase, "You mean you want me to say it again in a less elegant way?" Furthermore, the meaning of a poem may be interpreted in equally valid different ways. In fact, a number of readers of this book have pointed out to me valid, interesting, deep, beautiful, even fantastic meanings, interpretations, and other aspects of the poems that I did not notice myself. This section points out and discusses interesting aspects of the poems: alliterations, metaphors, symbolism, references to other phenomena and poems, internal rhymes, historical and scientific and other facts related to the poetic lines, and other interesting points that may not be easily recognizable to everyone. Poetic devices that are obvious are not mentioned. Discussing even the ideas that I do examine may not be the ideal course, since discovering such delights on one's own is a large part of the fun, growth, and being moved that result from the reading of poetry. Yet, since I intended this collection of my work to be read and enjoyed by inexperienced readers of poetry as well as experienced readers and poets, I am convinced that at least some readers in the former category will find this section useful. Moreover, since I wrote in this introduction that I hope to alleviate the problem of the irrelevance of today's poetry to the general audience and recapture some of that audience, and since some (not all) of the general audience I wish to interest in poetry are necessarily neophytes, this section is called for. This is especially true, since I stated that part of the problem is a lack of education of the general reader. I encourage the reader not to use this section before first thinking about and reflecting hard on the poems and reading them more than once. I put this section at the end of the book with all comments for all poems clumped together in one section, rather than putting comments on each poem immediately following it, in order to encourage the reader to carefully reflect on and re-read the poem before jumping to my discussion of the poem. To jump to this section without going through this exercise will rob readers of the possibility of discovering interesting aspects of the poems on their own, a valuable aspect for the enjoyment and inner growth that can come from reading good poetry. This section covers only some of the highlights, and does not attempt to explain every play on words, symbol, and other poetic device used, leaving much for the reader to discover on his or her own. And I encourage readers to make their own discoveries of aspects of my poems that delight them, and to make their own interpretations of my poems, both before and after reading this section, bearing in mind that my discussions of the aspects that I consider delightful or interesting and my interpretations are not necessarily any better than theirs. I stated in this introduction that I think scientific, historical, and other relevant accuracy is a desirable aspect of good poetry, unless there is a compelling poetic reason against it. There are some poems in this book that I think require explanations as to why they are accurate, or why poetic license is called for on this issue. I provide these explanations in this section. I also clarify meanings of poems that might incorrectly be misinterpreted as disrespectful or insensitive to religions, racial groups, and the like, in this section. There were a few poems that I had no comments on. To save space, I used Arabic numerals instead of spelling out numbers for stanza and line numbers. This "Author's Commentary On The Poems" section discusses the poems in the same order as they appear in the book.

This volume finishes with an "Alphabetized Index Of The Poems" by their title, followed by an "Alphabetized Index Of First Lines Of The Poems", both for the reader's convenience. The "Alphabetized Index Of The Poems" lists two page numbers for each poem, each in a separate column. The first column lists the page number of the poem itself, while the second column lists the page number of the author's commentary on the poem. It is this section that the reader should use to locate the latter, since I did not list its page number in the Table Of Contents, for that would have made the Table Of Contents overly cumbersome.

My poem, "Never Cry", has two versions, differing only in three lines (the third to fifth lines of the second stanza). One version is the original version that I consider the real version; it is more poetic, but suitable only to mature readers. I call this the official version. In the other version, I re-wrote the three lines that are for mature audiences only in a form which is suitable for people of all ages. I call this the family version. I wrote the family version so that the institutions I donated the poem to or submitted it to for publication in their newsletter or other publication could choose the version they want, according to whether they intend to display the poem in a setting where families would view it or not; hence, they have a choice between a more poetic version and one safe from offending the sensitive reader. The family version of the poem, followed by both versions of the three lines that differ from each other in the two versions of the poem, appears at the end of the discussion of this poem in the "Author's Commentary On The Poems" section. I donated this poem to Wolf Haven International, in Tenino, Washington. This is an institution dedicated to wolf conservation through educating the general public, and it has exhibits of live wolves. It also breeds wolves in the hope of re-introducing them to the wild , and lobbies for wolf conservation. They have this poem with my biography accompanying it prominently displayed on beautiful parchment in their gift shop. They are displaying the family version. The official version of this poem was published in two newsletters. One is Volume 10, Issue 1 (Spring, 2007 issue), of *Restoring Connections*, the newsletter of the Sky Island Alliance, which is based in Tucson, Arizona. Each issue of their newsletter has a theme, and this issue's theme is geology. It has other poetry in it. The Sky Island Alliance is an organization dedicated to the preservation and restoration of native biological diversity in the sky islands of the southwestern U. S. and northwestern Mexico. A sky island is a mountain range isolated from other mountain ranges. The ones they work to preserve have exceptionally high biological diversity. The other place that "Never Cry" was published is the Spring/ Summer, 2007 issue of *Arizona Wild*, the newsletter of the Arizona Wilderness Coalition, which has its main office in Tucson, Arizona, and works to permanently protect and restore wilderness and other wild lands and waters in Arizona. They are publishing it next to an article about wolf conservation. My poem's publication in *Arizona Wild* is the first time this newsletter has ever published an artistic piece of any kind, and is likely starting a trend, since their editorial staff has indicated they will probably now start publishing such pieces in future issues of their newsletter. I donated "Sky Wisdom" to the Chabot Observatory and Science Center, in Oakland, California, which is appropriate, because this museum is an astronomy and space science museum with telescopes for the general public to view the skies. I donated "Marriage in the Key of Ebony and Ivory" to the Stax Museum of American Soul Music, located in Memphis, Tennessee. Both of these institutions accepted my poems, but did not have them on display at the time of publication of this book, although they may sometime in the future. Both institutions are keeping a copy of the poem I donated to them in their archives.

The information in the above paragraph, and information on two or three other poems, appears in other places in this book, such as the "Author's Commentary On The Poems" section, or as explanatory comments directly above the poem that the comments refer to, or even in both of these places. This is redundant, but I chose to do it because I recognize many readers will not read all of the introduction or other sections of the book not containing the poems, and I consider the information important enough to warrant using this strategy to maximize the probability that the reader will read the information somewhere.

I am honored to present you with *Honor Thy Sow Bug*, my first book of poetry. It is my sincere and earnest hope that it will have help alleviate the problems I have spoken about in this introduction concerning the isolation, irrelevance, and poor quality of today's poetry, and start a process of bringing a wider audience to contemporary poetry. More than this, I hope that it starts or helps start a movement to re-awaken an interest in poetry in America today. I hope that it will have an impact and influence on contemporary verse, that it will influence other poets to write poetry that is exciting and relevant to the general public. I thank you for your interest in my poetry. I hope that you will be inspired and delighted, and find great pleasure and enjoyment from reading this book. I further wish you to learn and profit from it, and to be transported to a higher state of mental being. Enjoy.

THE POEMS

Midnight

Let's meet in the magnet of midnight,
Where the sea's fingers fondle the shore;
We'll be white in the candle of moonlight,
We'll be black in the ocean's red roar.
If you fear the maelstrom of midnight,
As the waves wash my sea-dreams of you,
Should too slight be a cloak made of moonlight,
Let's come in the dawn's silver dew.

Sinner's Rue

The sky was a thousand-eyed phantom,
The moon, an orange crescent torch,
The wind, blue death at red midnight,
When the two spoke their vows on her porch.

They vowed to be lovers forever,
And even in death not to part,
Should the sharp knife of fate ever sever
Either from life's throbbing heart:

The lover that lived on would never,
While he or she still had life's breath,
Take a lover, being faithful forever,
And would join the deceased upon death.

Their names were Janet and Thomas.
Green lovers must do what they must,
So he left with a kiss and that promise,
A promise she knew she could trust.

The wind whispered woe through the willows,
And the moon was devoid of its light;
Two lovers lay on two pillows
Two months to the day from that night.

They were Thomas and his other lover,
With a necklace of silver and blue,
With a pendant that held seeds within it
Of the flower they call Sinner's Rue.

With the false, gorgeous song of the Mocker,
The rising day's red on earth's rim,
The beauty of spring became blinding:
It was the hour for lies and for him.

The two made a plan that brash Thomas
Fulfilled in the shadows of night:
He dined with green Janet and poisoned
Her wine in the night's shades of white.

Then Thomas and his seedy lover
Buried young Janet that spring
By some flowers too faded for lovers,
By a creek that was too dry to sing.

His lover then went to the gravesite,
And wondered if life's ever fair.
She pondered the reasons for killing,
But never knew why she went there.

The wind blew like death at the gravesite,
And it shook her charm hard as it blew—
Shook the pendant with seeds of the flower
That is known by the name Sinner's Rue.

Thomas stayed close by his lover
Through the dawns and the doubts and the dew.
She now had less seeds in her pendant
Of the flower of woe, Sinner's Rue.

Nobody knew why it grew there,
Yet none could deny that it grew:
The flower of truth at her gravesite,
That goes by the name Sinner's Rue.

He went to the gravesite of Janet
To bid her a second goodbye,
And see if the grave he created
Could teach him a little of why.

The trees were cold white and cold silent,
All brown were the thistle and burr,
And the winter was barren and violent:
It was the hour for truth and for her.

All over the granite and Janet,
No plant blazed a bloom as it grew,
No flower, as if nature planned it,
No flower except Sinner's Rue.

The Sinner's Rue swayed in the sunlight,
It danced with the wind for its mate;
It seemed to speak gently and wisely
Of the way people set their own fate:

"Walk on the lighted path, always;
To yourself and the world, remain true,
So your fate, self, and fortune won't suffer
The pang of a blue sinner's rue."

Then his foot got caught in the foliage
Of the wind-dancing ghost, Sinner's Rue,
So he fell and his head hit the gravestone;
His skull was thus broken in two.

He therefore kept part of his promise,
And was true in his being untrue,
And joined Janet in death at their gravesite,
With the flower that's called Sinner's Rue.

For You

In the mist of a nectarine sunset,
In a sky that is changing its blue,
Like its colors, my changes aren't done yet:
My mind's moon is waxing for you.

You

You swirl me.
Your eyes are black diamonds
bathed in box turtle yellow
to make a delicious brown.
Your skin is leopard yellow
mixed with tiger-stripe black:
cat-perfect bronze.
Your charm is slow silver
tempered with turquoise.

Here's my creation myth about you:
Betelgeuse, Orion's red star,
fell to earth,
splashed into the Red Sea,
and made a haloed rainbow
around the moon on a misty night;
the rainbow dripped golden drops
that were blown to India,
where they made a tiger swallow its tail,
disappear, and re-appear
as a butterfly in California,
striped yellow and black:
a Tiger Swallowtail.
And out of all this beauty came you,
a fallen star,
rainbowed ruby of beetle juice red,
swallowtail yellow.

We gaze into each other's eyes,
our minds twirling
like two whirling dervishes,
spinning at the speed of night:
you, drunk with life,
I, drunk with you,
two drunkards with more wisdom than a sage,
this intoxication the only wisdom there is.
You swirl me.

As Bondage Ever Freedom Seeks

As bondage ever freedom seeks,
As bee is bound to bond to flower,
As sunrise seeks with lilac streaks
Eternity's best hour,
So seek I, seek I (one is two),
So seek I, seek I, you.
In love, since bondage freedom be,
(You are me and one are we),
The chains of love will set me free.
I'm partial to love
With all parts intact,
But when I lose my heart, I am
In fact
Made whole.
I'm bound to bondage in a love
That's bonded soul to soul.

Love Lies Still

Love lies in children's eyes
At the window sill:
Rhythmed by the rain drops,
Prismed window pane drops;
Love lies still.

Love lies in butterflies
On a flowered hill:
Reddish on the wing light,
Golden flash of spring flight;
Love lies still.

Love lies in peppered skies
Colored to the quill:
Calling feathered flight flocks,
Falling to the white phlox;
Love lies still.

Love lies in lovers' ties
Binding them until
They meet their end-of-mirth time,
Finishing their earth time;
Love lies still.

Love lies in Suzie's sighs
With her new-found thrill:
She said I'd be her one love,
More than just a fun love;
Love still lies.

Succession

My love and I walked hand in hand through fields of orange and amber;
We might have loved a longer time than lichens take, in slumber,
To burn rocks down from stony fuel to soil that's finely tempered,
But wrinkled rain announced her death with wind in dark December.
They buried her beneath our fields of gold and orange in summer.
The days I dwelt in amber grief were very few in number;
In much less time than nature needs to cover graves in clover,
I walked again the same grave fields, but with a second lover.
We should have loved a longer time than elephants remember,
But few days passed before I lost my life's last burning ember.
They buried me beneath those fields of raging rye and poppies.
As if to prove that fate can come in karma-coated copies,
In far less time than poppies take with rye to cover clover,
My second love walked those lost fields in love with yet another.

They stayed as one, this climax pair, unlike most lads and lasses,
A longer time than young oaks take to out-grow golden grasses.

Eyes of Chocolate

I'm the one that none can save:
Eyes of chocolate dug my grave.
I never knew, nor had a clue,
The magic that dark eyes could do,
For they were new, not what I knew:
I was raised on blonde and blue.

Why I fell for chocolate eyes,
I do not know, but can surmise:
Perhaps a rebel running wild,
I hated chains that caged a child;
Or maybe genes quite far apart
Are drawn by evolution's art
To make a child whose genes are mixed,
So better fitted, better fixed
To live and breed. Had I resigned
To stay the course with my own kind,
And match my eyes of blue with blue,
Maybe blue would have been true.
But maybe blue would too have led
To nightmares bleeding, damned and red
And maybe other chocolate eyes
Would have made my fortunes rise,
And let me see, through all the lies,
The truth behind the world's disguise,
And fawn on me, my chocolate tart,
She'd be my deer, I her sweet hart.
Yet when we choose a course or deed,
We never know where it will lead,
And speculating, "What if, then?"
Has never righted wrongs of men.
Whatever plan, however great,
Is subject to the whims of fate.

I was fooled by chocolate eyes,
Chocolate kisses and chocolate sighs;
The camouflage of chocolate highs
Helped chocolate lips hide chocolate lies.

My heart was deftly stirred in brown,
As I wore chocolate as a crown,
And fancied that I was a king.
And when I heard or saw a ring,
The only place my mind would dwell
Was on a finger or a bell;
In truth the circus came to town:
Its center ring contained a clown.

I found her with another love.
She lies with him, with ground above;
For with my fears, I'd brought a gun–
I melted chocolate like the sun.
Or so I fancy, so it seems–
Perhaps I shot her in my dreams,
In trying to kill the part of me
That holds the chocolate memory.
I might be in a prison cell,
Waiting for the death-bell's knell,
Or free and sailing to my death
(I quench my fire with every breath)–
In either case, my death is sure,
And soon to come, from losing her.

From the day that we first met,
Until the sun on chocolate set,
I calculated every move,
Designing each in time to prove
The surest route to happiness;
Blind reason, though, can spawn a mess.
It wasn't 'til the end revealed
Exactly what my plans would yield;
And now from me it's still concealed
At what point my fate was sealed.

To blind luck, our faults, or fate,
Or to our mind's demanding state,
Each of us is but a slave:
Eyes of chocolate dug my grave.

In the Glen

Each year the birds would call us
To where we should have been;
In spring it would befall us:
They'd call us to the glen,
And we'd go back again.

The songs, we so enjoyed them—
My young red love and I—
We endlessly employed them
To seek life's reason why,
As in the glen we'd lie.

"Green lovers," they sang to us,
"Come to the glen today.
Our songs," (the words rang through us),
"Will sweep gray days away;
Hear joy, and love will stay."

"Life was made for playing,
And far too brief's the play;
Love tends to turn to straying,
Flesh always turns to clay;
So live and love today."

One day we made a compact
Serving as a token
To birds and song, a contract,
Made of love, earth-spoken,
Never to be broken:

The grieving one would carry,
When one of us should die,
Straight to the glen and bury
The one whose eyes were dry
To there forever lie;

The living one, the lover,
When life should slip away,
Would join in clover cover
The lover in the clay—
There with the birds we'd stay.

If glen birds intertwined us,
Then we to them were bound;
Their songs would ever bind us
Together in the ground.
Our sleep would thus be sound.

And now your bird-beaks clatter;
You call me back again.
Oh, cease your senseless chatter!
I'm coming to the glen.
It doesn't matter when.

Beckoneeng Hill

Bright bloom the blossoms of Beckoneeng Hill;
They siphon their beauty from six purple down,
Where their roots find an anchor in love lying still:
They suck out the juices of young Molly Brown.

She was a beggar, all tattered and down;
She found food and lodging by love, skill, and will.
But don't dwell on paupers who roamed through the town:
I speak of the flowers of Beckoneeng Hill.

The Bluebells are church bells that ring the wrong tune:
They ring for a funeral for one dead too young;
They would have rang well for a wedding this June,
If fortune had seen that the right tunes were rung.

The Bleeding-heart droops and is broken in two;
Like the arrow of Cupid which shoots through one's heart,
Foxtails have pierced it and turned its red blue.
For tears, it drops petals–it's breaking apart.

The Bluebonnet, as on a head full of rue,
Blocks sun, heaven, light, and the blue of the sky,
But not lost love's pain or its not-of-sky blue;
Blue dyes my heart from the cast of the die.

Forget-Me-Nots summon the memory of love
Lost dark white in youth, and the bud of life gone,
And what men in tears all alone will think of
In the red of the night, longing for dawn.

The Aster lies flat like a fallen, dead star;
It hugs the dry ground and gets crushed as one walks.
A bitter wind grabbed it and pushed it too far,
And now it is lost in the Flax and the Phlox.

The Daylily's bloom, so gorgeous and brief,
Is like a young maiden, so pretty and proud,
Who leaves those who love her in blue-stomach grief;
With her music still in her, she's wrapped in a shroud.

The Sage and the Elder state Buddha's first truth,
And say, as the sun's flight increases their shade,
That in one of two ways comes the end of all youth:
All flowers drop quickly or gradually fade.

The Bittersweet paints a pale picture of life
On a canvas where laughter and joy must compete
With a rain made of blood, cold carnage, and strife;
It makes a good case life's more bitter than sweet.

The Locoweed says the whole system is mad:
Each outlives a person he loves, so is hurt,
And is loved, in an endless connection most sad,
By one who must watch him return to the dirt.

The Hemlock and Nightshade in triumphant bloom
Welcome grave lovers they cover in sleep;
The sleepers feed flowers from deep in their tomb;
From corpses to flowers, the life force must seep.

These flowers persuade with their rainbow of black.
I named them today as the heirs in my will:
I'll come here tomorrow and never come back;
I'll push up the flowers of Beckoneeng Hill.

Velvet Blue

Because he wore blue velvet
When she held him with a coo;
Because she held blue velvet,
She now wears velvet blue.

Blue velvet words were whispered,
And buzzed like a didgeridoo,
Until blood-red enveloped
A shroud of velvet blue.

The night was blue and velvet,
Warped with a reddish rue,
The night he died,
The night she cried,
The night of velvet blue.

The sky was blue and velvet,
It dripped blue velvet dew;
Deep in the mist the moonlight
Bathed death in velvet blue.

Velvet blue the evening,
Velvet blue their sighs,
And velvet blue
The "I love you"
That danced within their eyes.

And now where she is grieving
The purple sunrise screams,
While reddish Cardinals wing with
The orange of autumn's dreams;

Near Evening Grosbeak's yellow,
Green hues are held by yew;
So she completes the rainbow
With her blue velvet stew.

Wherever she may wander,
A sorrow sticks like glue;
The Universe
Vibrates the worse
When hearts are velvet blue.

And so for love's remembrance,
For her entire life through,
She plans to be in mourning,
While cloaked in velvet blue.

And I will wait a lifetime,
Yes, I will wait for you,
Through countless years
And endless tears,
Though you wear velvet blue.

My Only Song

My parents and my siblings
Were once my only song,
The only ones who loved me
Before you came along.
And so come join my family;
You should not be alone;
It's hell to see you suffer;
It grinds to dirt my bone.
People label crazy
My world, which they can't see;
They're jealous that you're loving
A "crazy man" like me.
Whenever someone loves me,
It melts my blue to green;
My gratitude transcends me;
Peace steams through my spleen.
It's rare that people love me,
But if and when they do,
I want to end their suffering;
I find I love them too.
You tell me you are happy;
My family said the same;
You say that life is precious,
But that's a common claim.
And so come join my family,
And I'll be your cocaine;
Be happy, don't be lonely,
I want to end your pain.
There's only pain in living,
There's freedom for the dead,
And that's why I am putting
This bullet through your head.

Springtime

In the springtime, in the springtime,
She sat lonely, sad, and still,
In the green and golden springtime,
He walked toward her on the hill.

He looked gallant dressed in azure,
Which ascended to the skies,
And the skies reflected azure,
Azure danced within his eyes.

The red wind wailed and whispered,
As it swept away her sighs;
She had springtime in her daydreams,
Last night's stardust in her eyes.

And her lips were ripe for kissing;
Her anticipation such,
She could almost hear his heartbeat,
She could almost feel his touch.

In the springtime, silver springtime,
On the bluebird's wedding day,
He walked toward her in the springtime,
Then he walked the other way.

Loving Words Are Flowers

Each word, every human-planted, love-tilled word,
sprouted from seeds watered by pouring brain,
rooted deep in the human soil,
follows its dendrite roots,
leaves the heart-touched lungs,
stems the teeth and tongue,
tied to its throat-stock,
petals the lips,
a flower in bloom.

There's Nothing You Can Do That Can't Be Done

Little sister,
why do you hug your doll?
She cannot feel,
she cannot return,
your love.

When the Woodlark Sings Deep in the Heather

"When the Woodlark sings deep in the heather,
And his song of green days can be heard,
Will we walk in the heather together?
Will we be as one with this bird?"

"When the Woodlark is back in the heather,
To sing to his love of his land,
With the change from white to green weather,
Will your heather heart be in my hand?"

I thus asked my love in fall whether,
If in spring through the heather we'd stroll,
If our hearts would be tied by a tether
Of a brown Woodlark making us whole.

Now the spring's come in plastic and leather;
It is tan-feathered tears that I cry;
I'm not with my love in the heather:
Would larks played on heather hearts fly?

My blue love and I are together,
But without any Woodlark's mint call.
No Woodlark sings hail in the heather.
It's been plowed and replaced by a mall.

Never Cry (Explanation)

I wrote two versions of "Never Cry", the next poem. The two versions differ only in three lines (the third to fifth lines of the second stanza). The version immediately below these remarks is the original version that I consider the real version; it is more poetic, but suitable only to mature readers. I call this the official version. In the other version, I re-wrote the three lines that are for mature audiences only in a form which is suitable for people of all ages. I call this the family version. I wrote the family version so that the institutions I donated the poem to or submitted it to for publication in their newsletter or other publication could choose the version they want, according to whether they intend to display the poem in a setting where family's would view it or not; hence, they have a choice between a more poetic version and one safe from offending the sensitive reader. The family version of the poem, followed by both versions of the three lines that differ from each other in the two versions of the poem, appears at the end of the discussion of this poem in the "Author's Commentary On The Poems" section.

I donated this poem to Wolf Haven International, in Tenino, Washington. This organization is dedicated to wolf conservation through educating the general public, and it has exhibits of live wolves. They have this poem with my biography accompanying it prominently displayed on beautiful parchment in their gift shop. They are displaying the family version. The official version of this poem was published in two newsletters. One is Volume 10, Issue 1 (Spring, 2007 issue) of *Restoring Connections*, the newsletter of the Sky Island Alliance, which is based in Tucson, Arizona. Each issue of their newsletter has a theme, and this issue's theme is geology. It has other poetry in it. The Sky Island Alliance is an organization dedicated to the preservation and restoration of native biological diversity in the sky islands of the southwestern U.S. and northwestern Mexico. A sky island is a mountain range isolated from other mountain ranges. The ones they work to preserve have exceptionally high biological diversity.

The other place that "Never Cry" was published is the Spring/Summer, 2007 issue of *Arizona Wild*, the newsletter of the Arizona Wilderness Coalition, which has its main office in Tucson, Arizona, and works to permanently protect and restore wilderness and other wild lands and waters in Arizona. They are publishing it next to an article about wolves. My poem's publication in *Arizona Wild* is the first time this journal has ever published an artistic piece of any kind, and is likely starting a trend, since their editorial staff has indicated they will probably now start publishing such pieces in future issues of their newsletter.

Never Cry

Your eyes, still shining mustard-moon yellow,
still able to awaken the walking dead,
are going out like two candles
melting their last bits of wax;
a bullet hole in your head
as wide as a dry desert river bed;
your head in my arms;
and a gun,
smoking like an extinguished campfire,
carried away by a running
marksman, manicured and masculine in his cowboy boots,
with bloody hands,
and an excuse of one dead sheep
(killed by disease).

Scapedog, we project our nature onto you,
create myths that misrepresent you:
when a man comes salivating on a virgin's breasts,
with schemes to suck on her Romulus-and-Remus-like,
and penetrate her,
thoughtless of love,
we raise our snouts,
dangle our tongues,
and howl, "   !"
When we tell our children fairy tales
of villainous, deceitful
predators of hairy-chinned little piggies,
grandmothers, and
little girls, red and innocent in their riding hoods,
we lick our chops,
bear our teeth,
and huff and puff, "   !"
When our sheep and cattle die
from brutal conditions leaving
stress, starvation, and disease in their wake,
or when buffalo, elk, deer, antelope disappear
in silver gun smoke,
we lower our heads,
raise our lips,
and growl, "   !"
When someone sucks
food straight into the stomach
like a vacuum cleaner
at relativistic speed,
we chomp on our teeth,
swallow our saliva,
and yelp that this is to "   " it down.

Without predators to offer us the possibility of death,
without the primal howl of evolution's night,
where is the wild in wilderness?
How will we awaken to our nature's connection to nature?
Or to the strands of spider-silk that tether us to the Universe?
Domesticated dogs can't awaken domesticated minds.

My wish for your race
is a
backward spell
on the
evil flow
of progress!

I could tear flesh,
rage like a mad dog
in anger about this bloody killing,
and howl madly
at the moon
about the need
to protect your species.
But that would be
taken as another excuse to kill
your brothers and sisters.
No: to defend your race,
I'll have to be
as gentle as a wolf.

Another Song

Cicadas are silent in summer,
They sing in the spring no more.
And earth has a different drummer
More noisy than before.

Cicadas don't sing in the summer;
They're nature's only sound,
For nature has become dumber,
And now they sing from the ground.

They sing in the winter and autumn,
Under a blackened moon;
They sing from a dry lake's bottom,
Alone, so way out of tune.

The frogs, toads, birds, and crickets
That used to light the spring
Are gone, along with the thickets,
From which they used to sing.

Cicadas sing at midnight;
The spring is mute and dead;
There's poison in the sunlight,
The midday sun is red.

The beasts that are taking the art out
Of song with cacophonous sound,
Are cutting the earth's green heart out,
Yet soon they will be downed:

Just as they kill all the others–
The singers, their songs, and the trees
(They need these, their sisters and brothers)–
They'll die with the forests and seas.

Then in time, without two-legged rat-forms,
The reign of death will dissolve:
New singers, with plants for their platforms,
Will rise from the slime and evolve.

Then cicadas will sing spring and summer,
With new species that nature has drawn.
With the breeze through the trees as a strummer,
The music of earth will live on.

Gaian Slumber

Queen, your ocean dreams are green!
Cheeks of cockled whelk,
Hair of tawny kelp,
Eyes of molten emerald quiver,
Hands of abalone silver,
Suspended by an icicle
Above the bitter sea, you dream
Of calico crabs in mouths of singing sharks,
Parrot fish that swim in parabolic arcs,
Purple-frosted stars and humming nights,
Terse virgin indigo and urgent white!

Queen! You're lost in forest dreams.
Waist of woven, winnowed laurel,
Limber legs of shaded sorrel,
Your mind seduced by crystal mandolins,
Songs of blue-tongued, saffron dragons,
Moths in sloth fur, fluorescent ocelots,
Poison arrow frogs with purple spots;
You sleep and dream
In seething mirth.

Awake!
Your children are destroying the earth!

Gold

A new day's love can now unfold:
The sun comes up with a dawn of gold.
River of orange and sky of green
Come to a sum that's a golden mean.
Quiet and quick, the artist, sun,
Paints the clouds with a golden run,
Melts the sky, so it drips free
To golden fish in a golden sea.
The wind blows poppies, yells and yields
To golden bees in golden fields.
An eagle's golden talons hold
A mouse of grasses, mouse of gold.
A golden pond in a painted scene
Is lit by a torch of Mallard green.
Though when day dies, the gold orb's lost,
There's a reply to the dark and frost:
Though gold can't stay, it comes back soon–
The one-eyed night sports a golden moon.

Earth Drums

Wet petals glisten,
Flutter and dance
Over the ground's percussion,
As they drop their drumbeats
To the earth.

Tears of Ecstasy

Since tangerine maples shade hunting wolves' heads,
Since forest-floor gardens are tinted with reds,
Since rain-rippled redwoods help ferns shelter frogs,
Since streams seethe with steam deep in pollywog bogs,
Since snakes come in colors da Vinci can't match,
Since Robins' eggs sing for their meals when they hatch,
Since from beggar to Buddha, we're creatures who cry,
Green ecstasy's tears are filling my I,
For star-dappled sea slugs, for plum-brindled sky,
For all nature's beauty, I burst, and I cry.

Dawn

Rainbowed sunrise flame adorning
Sky of red and purple light;
Light as down the downs at morning,
Mourning not the death of night.

Crystal-coated petals brewing,
Wooing sun, as diamonds wane,
Warn the bees that it's been dewing,
Doing what makes rainbows reign.

Light that floods a green cathedral
Through its windows, framed by leaves,
Leaves the leaves so tetrahedral:
Golden beams with silver sleeves.

And these beams are ever-changing,
As they light the leaves and wood;
Would they'd cease their rearranging,
Saying dawn won't stay for good!

Sky-bound mountains are contenting
Eagles slyly flying by–
"Bye," they cry, while they're lamenting
That this dawn should ever die.

During all the eulogizing,
As the thrasher feeds her son,
Sun is saying, as it's rising,
"What makes dawn break and brake is one."

Thus, while here the dawn is dying,
Dyeing skies to blue from gold,
Just beyond, the dark is crying,
Sighing, "Dawn will soon unfold."

In any given spot, revolving,
Waiting through a day and night,
Knight or knave, with mind evolving,
Knows what's dark in time is light.

Turning earth will never sever
Dawn from time, itself, or sky:
Forever dawn is somewhere–never
Ever-dying dawn shall die!

The Glimpse

I saw the world in a brave new shade,
Wisdom white hot in a grassy glade,
Unplugged from plastic, falling toward stars,
Kissing green Venus, free from red Mars,
Blood dripping freedom (all races bleed red),
Fresh with lust, as newly wed,
Truth being sculpted as rocks in streams,
Partly substance, partly dreams,
With love in all and all as one,
A timeless peace kissed by the sun.

Affirmation

Earth screams, melts, and answers
far and why.
I can hear the stars burn.
I feel venom move through,
permeate the black air
of an indifferent, purposeless Universe.
I see nothing living
that doesn't suffer:
Even the saint tastes Hell,
even the most fortunate feel fortune's fury,
are wounded by fate's flesh-ripping arrows,
experience Buddha's First
Noble Truth.
I fancy the world
expresses its piercing
pain in the wolf's howl
at a rouge moon
obliquely reflecting
a dying sun
at strawberry midnight.
Creation melts to zero.
A butchered forest cries
to a bitter sky
of humanity breaking nature
and its pact with it.
A tortured rose withers in reality's desert,
reminding that death is the fate of all,
even the Universe,
for liquid time will freeze solid blue,
darkness will rule.
The worm eaten by
a starving child devours his stomach.
And this above all:

the most constant and reliable
truth is
humanity's inhumanity.
My scorched tongue
asks the Universe:
"If some loathsome law coerces existence
to appoint suffering
monarch of its bitter core,
isn't nonexistence
preferable to
eternal agony?
Why is there something
rather than nothing?"
Silence.
As if it wonders whether I
have ever seen
a desert rose,
heard a wolf howl.
Then the wind comes and strokes my face
and answers me with an embrace.

Metamorphosis

My crankshaft has cracked in the Outback;
I can't hide my fear in my hide,
Alone out with you in the Outback,
My Aboriginal guide.
It's ninety-nine miles if we walk back
To the nearest town that's around.
I did not come here down under
To go down under the ground.
We may have to stay 'til the desert
Blackens its last shade of blue,
And I from a throne of white lilies
Am dependent on primitive you.
With endless sand as the where-there,
And Dreamtime forever when-then,
I would eat kangaroo blood and insects,
I would not see Seattle again.
If I can't come back out of the Outback,
From this desert where I can't survive,
If I must fight the night in the Outback,
The morning won't find me alive.
If I must remain in the Outback,
For even a part of the night,
I'll shiver from wombats and dingoes
Until I am dead from red fright.
If I can't get back out of the Outback–
In the desert there's nothing to do–
My boredom and rue will unglue me,
My whiteness will sink into blue.
Our nature is naked in nature;
Society's cloak's a sweet lie;
In front of the mirror of the Outback,
I'd see me so seamy I'd die.

The crickets and frogs are now singing
Like a chorus of crimson and cream.
The sunset is melting the desert
To palettes as true as a dream.
The light, as it's bringing down Dreamtime,
Reflects us, connects us as kin;
It places the red of the desert
As a kangaroo hue on your skin.
If I can't get out back from the Outback,
And must spend the night here with you,
If I must spend some days in the Outback,
Play me your didgeridoo.

Transcendence

Deep in a wood
In moon-lit snow,
Near where I stood,
I saw a glow

At my eyes' height,
Within a tree–
A whiter white
Than snow to me.

Its feathered claw
And yellow eyes
Fast dropped my jaw
In white surprise.

The mind denies
Both peace and ease
And classifies
All that it sees,

From cold to hot,
From fish to fowl;
And so I thought,
"A Snowy Owl."

This could have been
A moment of
A thoughtless Zen-
Enlightened love.

But thoughts that grasped for phantom categories
Made me blind
In my snow-melted
Mind.

I became
disconnected from
the rhythm of white
and nature, my nature, now snowless in snow.

I had to have a verbal label
up in my head
above my wherever heart lost
in the snow down,

far from the feather-rhythm of the owl and its yellow sun-eyes
and trying, thinking, panicking,
forgetting the perfect structure of snow-
flakes,

and growing ever more discordant,
controlled by my thoughts that ran me, I was
falling like snow,
and then suddenly the snow flakes

Hit me word-
Less and quiet!
Then my mind became
Deep winter white.

The need for words
Now flew away,
Like snow and birds,
I knew the play

Of life and love.
The white owl's eyes
Met mine above
My soul, now wise.

The owl and I
Were fused as one,
And I could fly
With eyes of sun,

And leave my rut
In feathered fun
Because of what
The snow had done:

When I had cried,
"I lost my will,"
The snow replied,
"Be still, be still."

Once upon a Cloudless Sulphur

Caterpillars crawl unconscious,
Even of the plants they eat,
Making juice erupt as pus does,
Where their jaws meet sweet, green meat.

As these juices flow from phloem,
Larval markings steal the show:
Their beauty is a colored poem;
But of this they never know.

Growing worms, like human egos,
Feed themselves and never quit;
Never knowing, as the tree grows
Skyward, they are part of it;

People-pillars think their egos
Are their wings, should never cease,
Falsely thinking they're amigos;
Egos are their Golden Fleece.

Yet a few in meditation
Spin a silk and gold cocoon:
Egos bow to transformation,
Buddha nature wakes in tune.

Both eyes closed while looking inward,
Third eye opens to what's true;
Skipper guides the vessel windward,
Polyphemus sees anew.

Sarcophagi of ancient Egypt
Sported pupa-plated lids–
Each a skyward-voyaging sea-crypt–
Boats in shapes of chrysalides

Took the pupae gods were snatching–
Wrapped cocoons in mummy cloths–
To eternal life for hatching
Into Sphinxes that are moths.

Whether Elfin, Monarch, Lady,
Nymph or Admiral, take a clue:
If you'd turn a mind now shady
To the light, know well, if you

Swallow tales of transformation,
Guide your fate as larvae do
To a transformed incarnation:
To awake, your death is due.

Every living being's a martyr:
Death is needed for a birth;
Death of larval Rambler, Satyr
Makes wings hatch that gild the earth.

Even Hermits have to face that
All must wear a Mourning Cloak;
Every ego must embrace that
It must die to break its yoke.

Life's and ego's great dissolver
Births the butterfly inside,
Makes red Death a red revolver–
Death commits its suicide.

Every worm that would awaken
To a true life has to die;
Once the larval life is taken,
Transformed soars the butterfly.

Once upon a Cloudless Sulphur
Wings of bronze and gold emerge,
To a sky of Purplish Copper,
Insect-Buddha's colors surge!

Reflections of Moondrops on Whispering Lake

Reflections of moondrops on Whispering Lake
Show that our world's made of dreams, as they snake
Through the water, presenting the world
On a mirror waves have altered and nature has twirled.
They teach us how often we get ourselves caught
Into seeing the world the way it is not.
A branch breaks a moonbeam to six specks of white
That flash, as waves move them, like fireflies in flight.
The shadows in sun of the broad trunks of trees
Weave on the water with each changing breeze.
They lie on the water, we lie in the mind:
We're chasing the fireflies the sun left behind.
We see through dark water with murk and high waves;
We watch Plato's shadows dance in our caves.
The seeker of truth has a lesson to take
From reflections of moondrops on Whispering Lake.

Follow the Light and Where

Follow the light and where
no shoes
moccasins if you must
bear feat of walking with
bare feet that touch earth
bear feet with claws that dig for truth
unburying it
eat it like
berries
swallow and digest it
until it is part of you
follow the moccasin must
get lost
in the wilderness that you may find
your way home
Follow the light and where

Follow the light and where
why not
knot that truth that nature bears
not that "truth" society's robots repeat by rote
not that truth is not in you
if you can see the trees for the forest
find your nature in nature
Follow the light and where

Follow the light and where
the drum
beat of the shaman beat
conformity
beat a path back to
beet wheat
corn squash amaranth

at first cultivation and before
when we antelope danced
slept with wolves
worshipped sun and earth
truth was truth was truth was
snakehawkmammothsunmoonearth
(we hunted and gathered almost all of our history
into stories)
Follow the light and where

Siddhartha Gautama

Siddhartha Gautama went out in the dark;
He lost himself found with now here to park.
He emptied his head on the lotus back Om,
And sat in a whole where his I's couldn't Rome.
Wh'n h' was th' tr'' grow, ask'd, "Wh'r' did th' 'e' go?
But if all is the void, it's best that eye know no."
Siddhartha Gautama went out in the dark;
Thought life's a wise owl, but found it's a lark.
Was small as an elephant, big as an elf;
Went looking for God, found only himself.

Zen Meditation on the Nature of Reality

The Way
to Shambhala

Come Nineveh, come Tyre,
come Jerusalem, come Rome,
come humanity, come home
to a red wolf winter,
to anything you hate or fear
that you see in the mirror.
There is business to tend to in you.
Shine a light
on your dark side.
We drown ourselves in trivia
to avoid looking inward;
we keep too busy to do
anything real.
Our biggest failing is our inability
to be content in an empty room.
The entertainment and things we seek are distractions
from coming to dwell in our home that dwells in us.
You cannot leave your home until you are in it,
nor know your path without a starting point.
I have traveled far in my room;
stay home and see the world;
arrive without leaving:
you are
your path.
You don't have to look out the window to see the grass.
You can't get there without a here
and a hear.
Would you go to
the moon?

You do not know
the earth,
your home (you're not home),
nor yourself.
Why would you travel to India to know
a sage,
when
the answers are in
you?
Who's your guru?
Spell it: G-U-R-U?
Let the sage be
you.
Come home.

This Water

This drop of water was in
the throat of a thirsty Tyrannosaurus after it dined on a Triceratops,
Babylon's gardens, hanging and dripping,
the Pacific Ocean carving a rock sculpture at Big Sur,
the red rain that washed over Aboriginal rock carvings on Ayer's Rock,
bacteria frozen in Antarctic ice for two thousand years before reviving,
the breath of a Tibetan Lama,
the piss of an Andean Llama,
a pool in a bromeliad in a Costa Rican rainforest canopy
    where a Poison Arrow frog tadpole swam,
the lichen on a rock in the Zen garden at Kyoto's Ryoanji Temple,
the tears of a forgotten lover who died for love,
a Bengali beggar's golden sweat,
a bucket at one end of a wooden stick on a Zen master's shoulders,
the black rain that fell on Hiroshima.

Reel Whiz Dumb

Real wisdom is crazy.
I said: reality is crazy.
Wisdom and insanity go to get her
As sure as
Water is always found with water because
Wisdom always contradicts itself:

Embrace the world that you may have a path,
But renounce the world to avoid tripping on the path.

Silence is the most eloquent form of speech.

Develop your ego in order that you may transcend it.

Embrace others that you may find yourself.

Form is emptiness;
Emptiness, form.

Light, illuminator of the Universe, is
Both particle and wave,
Yet neither wave nor particle.

Abandonment of all viewpoints is the path to truth.
That's a viewpoint.

The path to truth is the realization that
The journey to truth is pathless.

When you try to know it, you are departing from it.
When you depart from it, you are starting to know it.
Have a nice journey.

To reach enlightenment, be, hear now,
One who gives up all desires.
Should you have the desire to give up all desires?
Or should you have no desire to give up any desires?

Someone told me that this poem has two important truths.
He forgot the first, but he told me the second.
I'd tell you the second, but I forgot it.

The statement below is false.
The statement above is false.
Therefore, the two statements above are true.
If both statements true, they're both false.

Speak to the sage that the fool may hear.
Speak to the sage that the pine may hear.

He who knows does not say.
He who says does not know.
What is real wisdom?
I do not say.

Meditate, Tiger

Meditate, tiger,
eyes of the night,
there's oil in your dreams.
Meditate, tiger,
full of the not,
frozen in zero,
fluid in the infinite;
free us from the smoke of opinion,
the accepted axioms of society.
Meditate, tiger,
claws of cold fire;
truth is leaving us at the speed of death;
we dwell in the dust of dead rhymes.
Meditate, tiger:
a person could lose everything
in the flap of a duck's wing,
shattering it into a thousand pieces of June.
Meditate, tiger
in a symphony of agate.
Draw little sips of wind.
Open me that I can see my own eyes.
Let my fate be less under the wind's dominion.
Meditate, tiger!
Devour me
orange and black
that you and I will be one,
like fire and smoke.

Unreflecting Moon

Dark is the moon at the break of day:
It looks like a sphere made of night.
Dark is the moon when the sun holds sway,
As it stares at the white sun's light.

Dark is the moon in the dread of the night
With never a hint of a ray;
The full moon is black when it cries to be white,
And cannot reflect on the bay.

The moon wanders dark as if in eclipse,
Though no shadow is shading its zeal,
And the stars appear scrambled and misguide our ships,
As we fish and lose sight of the real.

The dark moon makes a cacophonous sound
That vibrates between our ears,
And people are lost, and fancy they're found,
And the world is not as it appears.

The darker the moon, the more people seek
Things of the world and want more,
And the more things seems straight when they're really oblique,
And the louder the cries are for war.

The moon will be dark until we awake
And observe our minds as an art;
Until we are silent, and once again make
The connection we lost to the heart.

Clay

I walk upon these fields of clay;
A shaman walked this path one day;
A dinosaur, in former times,
Carved out this path into new rhymes.
Though many fate drops make the mold,
Each traveler made a sculptor's fold
That bent my path a little bit.
And though my path is dimly lit,
I'll light my mind as I walk through,
And keep a course that I think true,
For other molders of this clay
Will walk this path I mold today.
Though they may think their will is free,
It's now being partly set by me.
And if I love and try to aid
Those who walk this trail being made
By all the life that walks on it,
I'll more than change the path a bit:
I'll feel what singing Sky Larks feel,
And be awake to what is real,
And know, no matter how distinct,
That everything that is, is linked,
That only one grand web was spun,
And that my path and I are one;
I'll feel the joy of Peter Pan,
And I will be a better man,
For all who walk a conscious way
Know, like our path, we, too, are clay.

Do Due Duty

Go to the saffron city with its melting metal
and broken doors:
to the poor and hungry,
give bread and music;
the illiterate,
teach to read, write, sing to cedar waxwings;
young girls, innocent and fragile,
save from slavery and pimps;
the fading forest,
reeling reefs of crumbling coral,
wolves howling in pain with less voice
than when earth was a greener green,
secure their preservation;
seek, too, the rich who cling to their wealth,
even as they hear starving voices shriek,
for the poorest of the poor are those who lack compassion,
the most impoverished are those who lack wisdom,
the most unhappy are the greedy;
they are the ones who need your help the most:
awaken them.
Go, and help any of the crying voices that need it:
they cover the earth ten times precious;
the sky is black and weeping,
the sun bleeds.

Go, and do good.

The Key

The key
to happiness
is not
to get what you want,
but
to want what you get.

The Way They Look

The foolish think at how they look.
The wise look at how they think.

The Sky Was Silent and the Moon Was White

The sky was silent and the moon was white.
Silence, passageway to wisdom,
named the name that can't be named.
Sky-silence silenced me,
my silence found infinity:
silence was sound.
The sky was silent and the moon was white.
The sky was so quiet I could hear the stars sing;
I became blind enough to see
moon truths in a mute poem,
washed in white and why.
I heard the harmony of a Universe
that stops at nothing:
infinite, without boundaries,
or
finite, with boundaries
and nothing beyond.
Nothing and infinity:
both are beyond
our grasp,
ensuring our fire of understanding
can never consume all that is.
Yet, in moon-sky intoxication,
I saw
if we can understand
the silence between the sounds,
the white between the colors,
we have a chance of awakening.

The sky was silent and the moon was white.
The white was at once nothing and infinity,
colorless white in all-colored light:
white thus connected to the black of night.
I merged with the sky, so
the Universe had an eye to observe itself.
And how did I have such insight that night?
By having a moon-sky mind.
Silent and white.
Silent and white.

Mined

The human mind is a load and lode,
And to *mine* the gold, one must *mind* the gold.

Sea wind sea water sea waves sea
woe to the mind that can knot sea
the flow of red
ocean in its motion.
Oh, wind oh to
the inner dance that wakes me from
my dreamy trance,
breeze me
faster, the disaster
is unmined,
unminded mind;
let my essence be
my find: my heart's the troll, I'll fish for
soul. Brain waves kiss, sculpt
the shore; presence preserves
its core; where I focus forms
a locus, where nerves make
a guild that helps my mind
build new wisdom ways
to form what stays, and upon witch I
can fast hitch
my mind
and heart,
my inner art. Wind-sea
brain, whether
vain, you wholed the cay to
waken me.
Brain kelp, you
help me to sail free and,
placid, sea
why I must learn to swim in the see
within.

Waves and Tides

Waves don't know the wind,
which ceaselessly drives them
home.
Tides don't know the moon,
which pulls them ashore
and away.

Tell Me No Lies

Plug my ears with cotton,
cork my eyes with candy,
jam my nose with syrup,
cram my mouth with popcorn,
and tell me lies about my death.
Tell me the night is good.
Cotton candy syrup popcorn death good?
No: plug, cork, jam, cram me with no lies about my death.
Closing my eyes to death won't keep the reaper away;
soothing water douses truth.
Life is a short spark in eternity.
Knowing this allows me to live with the fervor of a salmon
    seeking a spawning stream.

Wad my ears with feathers,
pad my eyes with chocolate,
fill my nose with nectar,
pack my mouth with sugar,
and tell me lies about my life.
Tell me I'm right and good.
Feathers chocolate nectar sugar life good?
No: wad, pad, fill, pack me with no lies about my life.
An unexamined life is limited and desperate.
Let me know my shadow as well as my sun.

Wrap my ears with paper,
plate my eyes with plastic,
paint my nose with plaster,
stuff my mouth with silver,
and tell me lies about the world.
Tell me all's bright and good.
Paper plastic plaster silver world good?
No: wrap, plate, paint, stuff me with no lies about the world.
The sky is the sky, regardless of any star's philosophy.
I cannot right wrong
If I think wrong right.

Soak my ears with passion,
seal my eyes with wisdom,
load my nose with caring,
gorge my mouth with beauty,
and tell me the truth about reality.
Tell me my sight is good.
Passion wisdom caring beauty reality good?
Yes: soak, seal, load, gorge me with truth.
Give me the orange
power to see both the doughnut and hole.
Truth is the chisel that allows us to sculpt the world we want.
My greatest desire is that the world have more
passion, wisdom, caring, and beauty
because of my red talon life.

The Magpie

Three magpies perched above a man
Who'd died one plum-red night.

One magpie said, "I think I can
Improve a bit our sight.
For of our shining feathers three,
The green and black and white,
The most important one that we
Bear on our wings is green.
For green is everything that's real;
It's all that's touched and seen.
Men pray to God, but seek the meal,
And toward the gold they lean;
They speak of spirit without zeal,
And chase what's on the screen.
This man's watershed was full,
It overran the earth;
The sheath that held his sword was whole
With riches, land, and worth.
He flourished in the worldly game,
And had a silk-skinned wife.
He soared, like magpies fly, to fame;
He played the magic fife.
So sell the spirit, keep the gold,
Grab what's solid and concrete;
That is real which one can hold,
The part of bone that grips the meat.
These are the things that set us free,
And make our burden light.
Green's what counts of feathers three,
Our green and black and white."

The second magpie said, "We must
See deep into the night.
White is consciousness, so trust
It fills our minds with light.
White's the light that lets us see
Ourselves with inward sight:
The best of all our feathers three,
The green and black and white.
This man achieved his wealth and name
Through magpie-mocking flight.
From his plane his bombs would maim,
Which he thought fully right.
He brought death to man and bird,
But questioned not the fight.
He died before he heard the word
That past his nose, there's sight.
He was his plane that he made sink
Into a lower plight.
He had thoughts, but did not think;
And from his lofty height,
He never saw the shades of jay,
Only black and spite.
He slept through night and slept through day,
Supine or upright.
What good are green, wealth, power, fame,
If one can't fly the kite?
That's why I say that white's the aim
Of green and black and white."

The third bird then spoke from the hip:
"You both are partly right.
But black stands for relationship,
Connecting day with night.
That is why it's number one
Of green and black and white.
This man knew not his wife or son,
And nothing of life's bite.
He took no pleasure in his things;
He held them out of fright.
His possessions clipped his wings–
They owned and clamped him tight.
The world gets blurred through crowns of kings
From far too great a height:
Kings can't touch a common man,
Or see from his plain sight;
This limits friends in their life's plan:
Relationships are slight.
So, that is why I surely can
Choose the black of light
From the colors of our clan,
The green and black and white."

We need each of the colors three:
Each bird was partly right;
They must be balanced equally
To keep our brain-fire bright
With truth's united trinity,
And guide us in our flight
From lives lived out of synchrony
To love and wisdom's light.

This magpie man, like most today,
Neglected black and white,
So he spilled his crooked tray,
And fell into a blight.
He built a fortune out of clay,
And lived his life in sleep:
He thought green the only way,
The only shade to keep.
He wasted life, and left unseen,
The light not from the sun,
As he surrendered to the green,
And left his art undone.
His game of life was never one
With the world, just fright.
Of colors three, he now has none,
Except in literal plight:
They dressed him in a tux to stage
A play against the night;
He's buried under grass to rage,
Or wage a war on light–
A flightless magpie in a cage
Of green and black and white.

Brief Is the Time

Brief is the time that roses are red,
Briefer the time that blood is not bled;
Short is the time that tears are not shed.
Brief were the crowns that covered each head
Of kings who once ruled over subjects in dread;
Soon kings became subjects of roses instead,
Changing to food that the roses were fed.
Brief is the crown of power and fame:
Soon gone the player, forgotten the name.
Like fire, love, and laughter, the white of the moon,
Streaked sunsets of scarlet, the call of the loon,
Brief is the time that butterflies taste
Asters that wither, buckeyes that waste.
Go smell the roses that bloom in the bed
Brief is the time before you'll be dead.

the only enduring reality

tears in the fabric
of existence are
following the wind
in the river
of air that traces
the course blood wound,
in proving pain
the only enduring reality

So Human a Predator (Explanation)

I wrote two versions of this poem, one much longer than the other. The reason is that the point of the poem is made powerfully in the shorter version, without the need for all the stories of the people in the longer version, yet the longer one has imagery that I like. I present the shorter version first.

So Human a Predator (Shorter Version)

The black panther paces
ceaselessly,
burning a morbid path in his cage,
always returning to the same dark spot,
going nowhere.
He can't comprehend the bars.

So Human a Predator (Longer Version)

I go to the zoo to see
the black panther.
Black panther essence,
pitch-crow precious,
pulls velvet night through ether.

The zookeeper,
feline heart
stripped of fur,
life-long
has moon-pulled
her father's love.

Life-long,
he has cat-flat denied her.
She never gives up,
forever inventing
new rosette and dappled ways
to please him.
He never responds.

The shoe-black leopard,
melanin king,
black diamond,
stands before me.
I hunger
like a cat
that has not eaten for a week
to see a wild panther
roaming an Old World forest.

Last time
I came to
see this panther,
a popsicle-blue woman appeared,
begging donations:
"Research for a cure to
my son's incurable disease."
The doctors had told her: "Lion hopeless–
two months to live."
Still,
sunrise to sunset,
she sweated, begged, hoped,
until four months
after predicted,
her son set.

Her other son suffers
pure black feelings,
oppressive thoughts,
like a leopard without spots.
He refuses medication.
His mind is a maelstrom
of obsidian sunset self-consumption
of reverse-stroked-fur regret
for actions
in his melted ice cream past
that have no strawberry bearing today:
ponderings scratch,
preoccupations claw him.
He wallows in, gets swallowed by
cat-chasing-tail thoughts,
horses on a race track,
electrons zip-zapping
in his very nervous
system,
until he awakes to
the self-inflicted pain,
vowing never again to be sucked into this
charcoal whirlpool of bleeding emotion.
He'll overcome his neurosis
by shear sable leopard power!
After five yellow minutes,
or two black-spotted hours,
the pattern burns through his cerebrum again,
the cycle repeats.

The lampblack cat paces
back
and
forth,
pupils oval, saffron-eyed,
dignified even behind bars,
cage blocking forest majesty.
His pacing is driven,
like a tragedy
forced to its end-of-the-tail
conclusion.

A wild Christian
clutching a Bible
shouts at the air:
"You must be saved!"
Every day, he roars
at the heathen,
playing the bass buffoon,
lassoing the wind,
alone in the paved wilderness,
pacing back and forth
on the same path,
ignored in black leopard sugar,
then made butterfly sport of,
never saving a sole
soul,
but never giving up.

The ebony panther paces
ceaselessly,
burning a morbid path in cement,
always returning to the same dark spot,
going nowhere.
He can't comprehend the bars.

Human and Mole

The human is unlike the mole,
Which crawls in darkness in its hole:
The mole is blind and knows it's so;
The human's blind, but doesn't know.

Green to Green

Change green to green.
Make youth into a beard of ancient moss.
Choke nature until it coughs up pictures of dead presidents.
Convert innocence to envy.
Puncture verdant hearts until they're jaded.
Change green to green.

Dead Alive

Living dead,
lights out with heart beat, dreaming
in Disneyland,
walking dead,
driven by the wind;
grateful dead,
like middle America;
emotions range from
road rage to TV happy;
EEG registers, consciousness doesn't;
deep sleep with eyes open;
clueless as a cornstalk
to reality
that
having thoughts is not thinking;
with a fast, mechanical mouth
that says, "How are you?" when
robot eyes flash
"familiar face" on computer-brain,
or, "Oh, really?" when comatose ears hear
almost anything;
happy head dead,
frozen to television, hypnotized;
eyes wide shut;
repeating by rote what's repeated as truth.
It could take years to fall over.

Lament

Sons of Sol, cease your singing;
daughters of Gaia, dance no more.
Reality is the water that douses the fire of ecstasy.
Life is short, and lacks conviction;
death is long, and without art.
The rub is not that ignorance is bliss,
but that cognizance is pain.
The world may be right, but the mind is wrong:
blind evolution constructed our brains to wish
reality weren't real.
The laws of physics grate against our hearts:
natural selection molded us into creatures that fear the grave,
yet the night will come;
we would burn forever green,
yet our fate is gray;
we plot our destiny as if life were a chess game,
but forget all the pieces
are knights;
we would be Michelangelos who sculpt our fortune,
yet the wind is a better molder of our marble
than our scheming brains and grasping hands;
we worship cause and effect,
yet the Universe plays dice better than it plays chess.
We pull at our fate like ants
dragging dead grasshoppers,
but the fundamentals are
as immoveable as granite mountains.
We are as flies buzzing against windows,
desperately seeking the other side of the glass.
The primal fault is not redressed:
we want to grasp the wind,
and the wind is not solid.

Seasons

Proud youth has spring in its step, and green earth hatches;
There's naïve faith that any seed of hope soon matches
Worms transforming into silver butterflies. Belief
In immortality. Green innocence can fall
In love so easily. Flames burn hot and fast, and call
Reality a lie. Trees cry that spring's so brief.

Summer: hot nights, and the need to wonder why
Brings beaches, bikinis, baseball, and the reply,
"Why not?" Desire melts, but doesn't disappear:
Fever and flames cover the earth. Faith holds it together.
Naïve lovers believe nothing but sunny weather
Will ever exist. Blind time is all one needs to fear.

Autumn, and wrinkles in wind and night say time is
Running out: life has become a tornado whiz-
ing woo until your falling leaves you short, and you'll
Do it now or write your never will.
So right your will, though the wind blows ill,
And regret cools the changing colors of a fool.

Winter's winds cry zero on the mortal plain;
Sleep on the edge of chaos creeps to cries in vain
For even a vague promise that spring
Will come again. Snow white lies are told
Of a fire that burns beyond the cold.
If you've a song unsung, it is time to sing.

Awe and Wonder

As we live our lives
Of snake-eyed greening thunder,
We never know which petal
Truth is hiding under;
To think we'll find the final truth's a
Skyless silver blunder;
So, as we search for truth, let's seek
The opal awe and wonder.

Black

"The most beautiful thing we can experience is the mysterious.
It is the source of all true art and science."– Albert Einstein

Black, God how I want you black.
Black wind, black fire,
the panther's midnight pace,
moon eclipsing sun and certainty,
the endless path to truth.
Black tears, mind of black,
thoughts of dark silver,
brain of fluid melanin,
spleen's surrender to the fire of the unknown.
Black God, how I want you black.
Black truth, trance of black,
dark maze to nowhere,
puzzle with no solution,
ebony answers that birth new obsidian questions;
let truth stay black.
Black, I so much want you black.
Black space, black time,
their explosive birth,
black sculptor of the cosmos,
dark dance of Shiva,
I shiver that I want you black.
Black void, black God,
or godless sea of black,
caves of sightless fish,
coy truth hidden in coal.

Black, how much I want you black,
black how, black why,
dark rain of gypsy mint,
black sight, brain in shadow,
pillows of frozen lava,
black spiders and their linking webs,
the sea's sunless marrow.
God is the mystery,
the Holy Grail is the quest
for truth.
Embrace the mystery.

Sky Wisdom (Explanation)

I donated the poem immediately below, "Sky Wisdom", to the Chabot Space and Science Center, in Oakland, California, which is appropriate, because this museum is an astronomy and space science museum with telescopes for the general public to view the skies. They accepted it, but did not have it on display at the time of publication of this book, although they may sometime in the future. They are keeping it in their archives.

I wrote the stanza of "Sky Wisdom" that you see below the rest of the poem and separated from it by a dashed line as a tribute to the Chabot Space and Science Center, because I donated the poem to this museum. Other than this tribute, I did not intend it to be part of the poem, and do not consider it as such, for I intend this poem to speak more generally than it would if it highlighted a specific science center. I included the last stanza for those interested, but set it off from the rest of the poem with a dashed line above it to indicate that, except for the version in the Chabot Space and Science Center, I do not consider it part of the poem.

Sky Wisdom

People look up at the skies,
Though the land is close at hand;
They firmly direct their eyes
Far up from where they stand.

They strive to understand
The truths the sky can give;
Some even make our land
A better place to live.

But comfort in our world
Is not the reason why
They want the truth unfurled
From looking at the sky.

They look because they love
The beauty of the sky,
And mystery blazing above,
Burning far and high.

They look because of their love
Of knowledge, which is why I
Respect and think highly of
The people who look at the sky.

When they look with intent, and try
To discover the truth, they find
That the truths that dwell in the sky
Are the truths that dwell in the mind.

The better we know the sky,
Through our eyes and books on our shelves,
The better we know how and why,
And the better we know ourselves.

Philosophy comes from
The knowledge science supplies;
Of all of this learning some
Comes from the generous skies.

Our philosophy's improved,
Our wisdom can flourish and fly,
When some of the mystery's removed
By the knowledge we get from the sky.

And we can enhance our wonder,
And increase and enrich what we know
Of skies we love and live under
At the magical place called Chabot!

Winds of August

Winds of August do not care
If life, or whims of fate are fair,
That people suffer, hard and long,
The weak are trampled by the strong,
Green life is shortened by red death,
Or plum wine sunsets steal our breath.
August winds oft change their song,
Without regard to right or wrong;
These searing winds can bring down kings,
Soar a hawk, or clip its wings,
Bring love to a starving heart,
Give the lost a second start,
Fill a pauper's purse with gold,
Make the hottest fire go cold.
Winds of August do not know
The fortunes carried when they blow,
How they deeply change our fate,
And sear our hearts with love or hate.

Winds of August blew pale sails
Straight from Europe with their gales,
Bringing smallpox, spilling blood,
Building missions out of mud.
Turtle Island, in the fight,
Changed from red to windy white.
History changed by winds that blew,
Unconscious of the dice they threw.

Winds of August wrote a tome,
Built, expanded, buried Rome,
Blew away its pagan past,
Yet ensured it'd partly last,
Wafting pagan tales and creeds
Into Christian myths and deeds.
The winds blew Christ upon the west,
And Christian values to the crest,
Then blew these values down to Hell,
And left the label as a shell.
Beyond this creed's forgotten text,
What religion will breeze next?
None can ever surely know
What new creed these winds will blow,
The next strong faith they'll whiff our way
To replace one gone astray.
Or could Christ's teachings once more rise?
Could August winds blow Christians wise?

Blowing over lands of war,
Over fields of blood and gore,
They're unconscious of the dead,
Of the soldiers in their bed;
Though they go where sabers go,
Though they blow where bugles blow,
They never hear the bugle call,
Or see young soldiers when they fall,
Or hear the wails when women weep
For the soldiers put to sleep.

If random winds thus set our fate,
And we can only hope and wait,
If they don't even know we're here,
Or that they're blowing, far or near,
Then winds of August blow us ill,
Killing hopes we have free will,
And tell us how we came from mud,
Are made of only bone and blood,
And how to fate we are but germs,
That we'll end up as meals for worms,
And so our journey ends in sod:
They blow away our dreams of God.

Nature's Nature

Hero of a yesteryear,
Bedded in forgotten sands,
How the crowds that used to cheer
Sleep in treeless, weedy lands.

From earth to sky you burned with fame,
Then flesh made soil and soil made sod.
Folks soiled and soon forgot your name.
It seems impermanence is God:

The lily, nature's brightest bloom,
Fades before the fade of day;
Death and time are bride and groom,
And fame is made of sand and clay.

But does the sky not cry for you
When tears tap on your grave as rain?
Does not the wind remember, too,
With wailing sighs of wailing pain?

The wind wails with unconscious sighs,
And nature weeps, it's true,
Tears from dark, indifferent skies;
They weep, but not for you.

I've Known Oceans

I've known oceans
with tides more ancient than the crimson fluid in our veins,
seas whose waves ebb and flow with the same rhythm as
    our scarlet pulse,
oceans that bled
sea water that leaked into our arteries
before we crawled onto land,
with waves that roared, "No God! No, God! Know God
is time, blind molder of blood from mud, salt and water."
I've known oceans that know no God.
My blood is tide to an ocean.

I've known oceans
with billows synchronous with
waves on the surf-
ace of my brain,
in an electrical storm,
rising from the submerged, sunless sea of my subconscious,
home of dangling blue,
of mermaids of silver fire who could deceive the dead,
tangerine-voiced whales,
octopi dreams,
giant squid id,
gyroscopic dolphin dervishes;

this bottomless, black sea running my life,
controlling me as currents direct plankton,
decisions bubbling up
from deep sea vents,
thoughts and feelings as currents
from seaweed dendrites in the abyss,
hidden from awareness,
my control equal to a swimmer in a rip tide.
I've known oceans I cannot fathom.

I've known oceans
with algae-covered truths
in sable depths,
yet undiscovered
by those green to know them;
black seas with black coral puzzles,
dolphin sages concealing sea secrets,
whales that have plunged to the earth's foundations,
where hot volcanic vents rot unrecorded names and navies,
answers and anchors rust,
waiting to be discovered and polished,
increasing the size of the sea that's known
to be unknown.
I've known oceans beyond the see.

No It U Love

Edit DNA, Emit–wait,
for no man
evolves without woman:
sexes complementary,
like all fundamentals of
yin-yang, spirit-
dual Universe:
MOM and DAD
(MOM up-side down is WOW!),
flower-bee, proton-electron, predator-prey,
two as-
specks of light, part-
tickle and wave,
two strands double helix,
palindromic DNA sequences.
Can name no one man
who evolves alone.

Is each one of existence's complementary pairs
one entity with two aspects,
each the reverse of the other?
Is yin backward yang?
Is the Universe a palindrome?
Is a palindrome the container
for love? And time, Emit? DNA evolves
embedded in a palindrome?

Edit DNA, Emit–wait for no man,
for humans are not evolution's inevitable result:
dog, cod, doc, god as meme, earwig
passed natural selection test.

Was it a rat I saw?
Yes, no oozy rat in a sanitary zoo,
it co-evolved
with other species.
Rats live on no evil star planet:
evolution follows spiritual laws,
most fundamental (they emit time);
pre-ordained pat-
terns fly over the wholly sea
of Uni-
verse be-
fore play
of life results.
Evolve holds love in a backward spell;
evolvers rev love.
Go backward in time,
laws causing natural selection to
favor virtue still
apply:
rats lived on no devil star planet,
no devil lived on,
devil never even lived!
Do geese see God?
No: only a few humans are conscious
of the guiding spiritual laws.

Sums are not set as a test on Erasmus,
neither Desiderius nor Darwin's granddad;
rather, math describes
Universe's loving blue-
print, with time folding back on itself,
a quantum palindrome,
a circle (Universe: "I prefer pi").

Edit DNA, Emit—weight for no man
to shoulder (not a ton, not an ounce),
for it's evolution's job.
First evolve DNA, Emit,
from dumb mud:
G, T, add A,
can I attain a C?
Maybe add molecules from space
(and E. T. saw waste DNA?).
Edit peptide in DNA land.
Evolve prokaryotes, eukaryotes;
don't bar crab or any invertebrate;
Triceratops, giant herbivores
that diminish a local plant population (no garden, one dragon);
tuna, nut, bird rib;
diversify mammals:
camel in Nile, Mac,
dog, elk, cat, emu, ("me tackle God,"
says Emit, if evolution goes *that* far),
stack cats on;
let mammals compete
(alpha elk: "I tip away a wapiti");
evolve ecosystems:
God, wasp saw a dog,
gnat sums mustang up;
evolve all manner of species interactions
(may a banana nab a yam).
Swap paws for hands and feet,
evolve late fetal birth–
result: human;
evolve wolf-human mutualism,
dog domestication
(go, do, dog;
step on no pets, human,
though there will be some abuse:
God! Nate bit a Tibetan dog!).

All this through extinctions:
meteors,
tar pits (lion, O, puma, I am upon oil!),
volcanoes (deer gas? I disagreed).

On a Toyota? No!
Pro-
creation, evolution don't
fare well
on artificial, metal, plastic habitats.

Egad, a base life defiles a bad age;
doom an evil deed, liven a mood;
live not on evil, Madam, live not on evil
that your life will have harmony, not
harm on Y, nor X, chromo-
some. Some,
having lived ethically,
can say,
"Now I won:
no evil I did, I live on."
Even politics is subject to this, pal, in dramatic,
    spiritual complementarity:
no evil shahs live on.
Edit DNA, Emit,
wait for no man.

The Origin of Species (Explanation)

To write this poem, I took the last paragraph of Charles Darwin's book that presents his theory of evolution by natural selection, *The Origin of Species* (published in 1859). I added my own line breaks, changed some of the wording and punctuation a small amount, and changed some capitalized words to lower case, to make it into a poem.

The Origin of Species

It is interesting to contemplate
a tangled bank,
clothed with many plants of many kinds,
birds singing on the bushes,
various insects flitting about,
worms crawling
through the damp earth;
to reflect
that these forms, elaborately constructed,
so different from each other,
dependent on each other
in a manner so complex,
have all been produced by laws
acting around us.
These laws include
natural selection,
entailing divergence of character
and extinction
of less-improved forms.
Thus, from the war of nature,
from famine and death,
the most exalted object
we can conceive,

the production of higher animals,
follows.
There is grandeur in this view of life,
with its several powers,
having been originally breathed
by nature
into a few forms
or one;
and while this planet has gone cycling on
according to the fixed law of gravity,
from so simple a beginning,
endless forms
most beautiful
and most wonderful
have been,
and are being,
evolved.

Death

Oh, how I hate the death of dawn,
And olive youth and beauty gone!
I grieve that present will be past,
That nothing in this world can last.
Great granite mountains wash to dust,
The strongest bridge of iron must rust,
Even the most steady form,
Whose *persistence* is the norm
The stable proton–cannot stay:
In time, this also will decay.
The greatest foe I know is time.
What is the point of art or rhyme,
Reason, science, gentle rain,
Development of mind or brain,
Understanding why we're here,
All the things that we hold dear,
Understanding right from wrong,
Being moral, smart or strong,
Making laws or holding court,
Accomplishment of any sort,
Knowing what is false or true,
Or *any* deed that we might do,
Philosophy, or healing hurt,
If all of us end up as dirt?
Soon after birth, we start to wane;
Mortality's our source of pain;
The grave erases any gain;
Such brevity makes life in vain.

There is some solace, if you're wise,
Knowing every being that dies
Is replaced by young, new life:
We play the bugle with the fife;
Every sunset, every night,
Is followed by next morning's light.
Still, when dead, one's not aware
Of anything or anywhere.
When I'm dead, I will not know
That new green sprouts and youth still grow.
So I forever curse the night,
And question: Why this morbid plight?
Why can't the doe remain a fawn?
Why can't there be eternal dawn?

Fingers of Nightshade

Fingers of nightshade hide in the blue,
hide in the blue even,
even as awed as
intelligent life in
the Universe is
a merry-go-round turned by
beauty and love
are its music.
Even the deserts of night loom in bloom.
Beauty, fierce beauty, the apricot, apex, primordial truth:
flight of the Kite,
white of the night,
and all that's in nature by
nature is good.
All we touch takes
the spirit of gold
within, without
the curse of King Midas,
if only we open
our senses.
Nevertheless,
ever never will be:
fingers of nightshade hide in the blue
shadows of night, shade in the light:
the nightshade
can fade,
hide in the glade, or even
the green that leaves the trees,
and even as much of the green lives on
its fingers are
a phantom for rest for the rest of the forest.

The most mundane moment
is a miracle.
All around us poppy gold
glory and carnation
Paramecium splendor
paradise sunshine wonder
cinnamon and clove.
It doesn't matter bitter, salt, sweet, or sour,
or nothing on the table:
life is good;
it doesn't matter what's for dinner–
liver, onions, apples, ice cream,
empty stomach biting zero:
life is good.
I love the cat that walks under the June.
Life is a vermillion volcano
that erupts streams of diamonds:
a starling in starlight,
Saturn's silver
(silver rings shiver,
deliver a sliver of white in the slight),
a sundog, a frog bog,
a fogless indigo
lake that mirrors
night's charcoal
sky of shiny freckles–
reflections on earth as it is in seven
stars of the Pleiades.
Yet, though
mortality makes beauty more beautiful,
beauty makes death more morbid.

There is always a lemon with the peach;
every silver lining has a cloud;
one can't make a pearl
without irritating
the oyster.
The lemon-cloud is:
silver, oysters, blue,
peaches, pearls, me, and you
don't last forever.

I spell
the word
true
with sweet tea
and a rue:
fingers of nightshade hide in the blue.

last psalm

in a man-
go sun-
set in a tan-
ge-
rine sky
under a mush-
room
cloud crow-
ding the sea
gull's cry
cho-
king on child-
wren's screams
deep in an un-
clear raw
e-
motion, wheel
dye.

Duende

She sang with a voice of sunflower nectar,
with the sweetness of a dolphin making love to Athena,
voice of oriole orange,
tangled in flowering vines and angel's hair,
floating in pools of water in orchids in a rainforest canopy,
clothed in bird of paradise feathers,
housed in a bower bird's garden;
coral-covered mermaid
voice of several shades:
of octopus, chameleon of the sea,
of shells hermit crabs fight over;
she would soak her voice in sangria,
or lose it
in the ecstasy of a Picasso.
She had sung with a manicured competence,
but without
duende.

The audience was as mute as a windless cave,
except for a sarcastic remark
from a toreador behind
bottles of bleeding sangria,
"Ole!"

So she drank fire-water and sang a second time,
without lotion in her voice,
breathless,
voice of black fire;
tore the scaffolding off the song
to make way for a furious and fiery duende;
shred her voice, brought the wind down,
ripped a bird from her throat,
engaged duende in a saber duel,
her voice a jet of blood
as she sang with her voice of shadow,
with a ghost-fire duende,
brother of a black wind,
torn from the far side of the moon,
dredged from the sea's depths beyond the reach of light,
spinning in galactic black holes,
tangled in thickets sheltering tongue-flicking rattlesnakes,
dark voice of volcanoes and deep-sea vents,
lost in earth's bowels,
reverberating in dark and distant swamps;
dragging her wings of rusty knives along the ground,
her voice opening like a starving sea anemone
with vipers for tentacles.

The audience was as a waveless ocean,
stunned mute
to a silence of red platinum,
letting her know that she had transported
their five senses
to communion with the celestial.

Marriage in the Key of Ebony and Ivory (Information)

I donated this poem to the Stax Museum of American Soul Music, located in Memphis, Tennessee. They accepted it, but did not have it on display at the time of publication of this book, although they may sometime in the future. They are keeping it in their archives.

Marriage in the Key of Ebony and Ivory

This music's a marriage of chords black and white;
It grows ivory lilies in Harlem at night.

In Africa's jungles a rhythm was born;
It crossed the Atlantic in ships made of scorn.
Only the poor and oppressed with their rues,
Only the lonely, can master the blues.
So from hard beating, heart bleeding, so down,
The black and blue bruises blew blues a sound sound.
Ebony rhythm, still paying life's dues,
Was mixed in the cauldron for rhythm and blues.
With a large, liquid range from which it was styled,
Its songs were creative, throaty and wild.

Meanwhile, from those driving cattle out West,
With a home on the range, not much time to rest,
Came music that spoke of their loves and their wills,
Lilting and rolling, much like Western hills.
They would sing of lost sweethearts and call them by name;
Corralled just like cattle, their chords were kept tame;
They sang, though, like coyotes that howl at the moon,
Of life in a prison or in a saloon;
It made some folks wonder, between the blue bars:
Which has greater glory, our songs or the stars?

Snow married coal, and this music was born;
On the platters of Doo Wop, old patterns were torn.
Up on Haley's Comets, some claim came the start.
Holly was planted, and –Oh Boy!—gave such art!
Good Golly, Miss Molly, when a direct thrill
Was loved by young ivory, some parents grew ill.
"Eve yells, rips her clothes," so the headlines would say,
For the best voice of all had a pelvis with sway;
The blue-eyed young king sang a black-and-white key;
Fans got all shook up when he sang r & b.
Another King crooned on so cool in the coal,
A gnat who fused sweetly slow country and soul.
Some foolish "critics" complained as they frowned,
But couldn't chuck, bury, or vanquish the sound.
Black in the country, now none could deny
The marriage succeeded, the music won't die.
He hot; cay ebbs high, falsetto's his turf:
Sweet Little Sixteen in the sound of the surf!
Ebony ladies of talent were found
Who created with love a great wall of sound;
They sang crystal songs that reached a new height,
Produced by a ghostly, bright specter of white.
If surf music's written in ivory-white chords,
And Berry won smile-brain (who never rode boards);
With the help of sweet voices, and fill up once more,
(Will you be my baby? You've been it before),
Can Ronettes be muse for this greatest of men?
Don't worry, baby, Black guides surf again!

The music went over the ocean once more;
This time to Great Britain to set a new score.
The holly, the berry, the waters of mud
Influenced music that surged like a flood,
With chords of white blues and with this point to tell,
"We'll break ground and the rules, so sing rotten Hell."
With no satisfaction if slave to the rules,
They'd coat with brown sugar their new set of tools.
The blues fans clapped on to a great guitar skill,
And he creamed their blind faith that the yard birds sat still.
There's a place in the heart that this music would seek;
And it pleased many people eight days a week.
If music were liquor that never gets stale,
We fans of the Sixties all drank the best ale.

The most needed deed that could ever be done
Is bringing two races together as one;
This deed is too loving to measure its worth,
And nothing's so helpful to bring peace on earth.
Though marches, fasts, sit-ins, and speaking helped some,
The best success came from the strings and the drum.
And of all of the music from heart, mind, or soul,
None has united quite like rock and roll.

We'll dance to this union, we're not going back;
This music's a marriage of chords white and black.

I Dream of Ebony

Race envy,
and you'll always lose.
My skin in full light
bloom, privilege-born,
stomach, pockets
bursting, so it is
said. Yet I see riches
in hearts,
wealth in emotions
in African blood, but a poverty
of emotion in my heart,
being out of heart,
I dream dream,
I
  dream
        of
           ebony.

Down
in my dull ivory
tower, thought speeds, screams,
and bleaches emotion
white out
of existence.
Chattering head feels
no emotion,
just loco-
motion.
In an empty room of hard alabaster,
dream I dream
I
  dream
        of
           ebony.

Privilege is the thief of emotion.
Leaves can feed the tree only
if the sun shines on
them.
The leaves that feed the branches
are the ones that do the dances
and taste the wind.
Only the oppressed know
whether morning
dew is the tears of night
or sweat of a new day.
I feel the isolation
of an albino crow.
I dream I dream
I
   dream
            of
                ebony.

The oppressor is a prisoner of his own oppression.
The master is a slave,
the unjust jailer is a prisoner, barred
from emotions:
suppressing guilt suppresses joy and love.
From
the bower of Harlem
to
the garden of Soweto,
obsidian dances,
emotes, loves and cries,
laughs and fears, feels
anger, ecstasy, lust, alive.

Feeling is life.
My blank, pallid slate of
emotion has nothing
on the scoreboard.
My feelings are replaced by thinking
words:
"I am
angry, I
am happy."
I watch life
like a movie that I'm not in,
am like a robot
that is
a spectator of the human race.
The joke's on
me.
And I
dream, and when
I dream,
I
  dream
          of
              ebony.

In the deserts of White,
in the prisons of Beverly Hills,
on manicured lawns,
in shiny, pale, little mansions,
white wanes to wan.

I hunt for my heart,
but get lost
in my head, where
thoughts control me,
are noisy, painful, loud,
like slave-master's whips.
My blank heart on the other side of
my brain-dungeon bars
my emotion,
eluding on the dark side
of Luna, ticking
my life away.
Until I learn to shut
off thoughts
and emote,
I sleep,
and when I sleep, I dream,
and when I dream,
I
  dream
        of
            ebony.

Pieces of April

I have pieces of April
On a morning in May;
I have feathers of finches
That flew with the jay;
I've the map to Nirvana,
But can't find the way.

I have fragments of sun-
Rise at the end of the day;
A thousand black sunsets
Have faded away.
A God that forgot me
Cannot hear me pray.

I have fields of dead poppies
That withered to gray;
I see faded fuchsias
Above friends in clay;
I have pieces of April
On a morning in May.

I have cadmium moon dreams
That died in the day;
I've the bare night of winter,
Yet stars cannot stay;
I've the desert's scorched sand dunes,
Where once was a bay.

I've reflections of earthshine
From a life gone astray.
Our past is a dragon
That we cannot slay.
I have pieces of April
On a mourning in May.

Y Knot

Mary had a little lamb,
whose heart was white as snow.
And everywhere that suffering went,
the lamb was sure to go.
It fought against the empire, Rome,
which was against the rules.
The Roman legions laughed, and flayed
"the lamb-chop woolly fool."
Rome was angered when it stood
for justice and the poor.

<pre>
                    c
                    r
The Romans went to cross it out
                    s
                    s
</pre>

when they could take no more.
It taught of love and giving, yet
neglected something else:
It saved a lot of people, but
It did not save itself.

Jesus, How You've Changed!

Jesus, how You've changed!
Lord and stranger
to Your foulerers,
You were born of a version
antithetical to Your current form.
You were born again
a hateful fanatic,
demonstrating that man created God
in his own image.

One good fry day,
the Christ-shams cooked all Your love
out of You,
set You on across
a river of blood and
hate,
nailed loathing into Your hands and feet,
speared hatred into Your heart,
resurrected You on easter-
ly winds of black,
on a son day,
as the antithesis
of what You were,
antichrist, full of
venom and malice.

You were the advocate of the poor,
who said,
"It is easier for a
camel to go through the eye
of a needle than for a rich
man to enter Heaven,"
and,
"Sell everything you have
and give to the poor,
and you will have treasure
in Heaven."

You fought against empire.
Now evilangelists with divine connections
to You via their cell
phones broadcast Your new message:
You are despiser of the poor,
enemy of welfare,
lover of profit, empire, free-not-fair trade,
justifier of
avarice of the rich,
who declares the poor poor
because of lack of morals, discipline.
They print "in money we trust" on their god.

You once said, "Blessed are the peace makers;"
now Your war shapers
take Your name in vain
when they use it
to justify bombing the innocent
in war;
developing more power-
ful forms of weapons already capable of
vaporizing earth,
destroying all higher life
in two hours;
fighting endless wars
to nowhere, no purpose but
to defend freedom
of arms
merchants to
seek their Profit
that they worship so
deadly.
You have become their
Ares,
Mars.

Your tree is good,
but the fruit rotten;
"By their fruit you will know them,"
fails to hold true
when the fruit has been poisoned;
this is the only case when this wisdom fails.

Your transformers molded You into
a vitriolic hater of homosexuals–
it is a family
value to hate
gays, deny them
their rights.
Irony: gay marriage is to be
illegal, thus
the only legal gay sex is out of wedlock.

Your new molders have You saying
women do not
own their bodies,
are not entitled to freedom of choice,
are second-class citizens,
less than men,
unwed mothers should be sterilized.
Whither went
"Blessed are the merciful,
for they will obtain mercy"?

They have You advocating sex
education is not to be permitted in schools;
no birth
control permitted
of any kind,

as the world
population grows and grows and
devours our future, our earth.
Be fruitful, and multiply
that earth and its preservation
be fruitless, and divide
the spoils take dominion over earth.

They Armageddon claim
You'd say
the earth is here
to be exploited, despoiled for profit;
their god will destroy it:
why protect it?

If this is You,
then I am a lost sheep,
and
You are the shepherd
I shall not want.

But this is not
You.
I wish You to be
borne again on earth,
full of compassion and love
for the poor, an advocate
of world peace,
preservation of earth, its wild species,
protector of the planet,
metaphor
for love.
But then, turning
and turning in the widening gyre,
the falconers would come,
and,
seeing that their merciless molding of
You failed,
slouch toward Bethlehem, bow,
grasp Your white cloak, and
crucify You.

Red

Is the red on the flag the color of freedom?
Is the red on the flag the color of blood?
Is the color of freedom the color of blood?
Is the red on the flag the color of fire?
Is the color of freedom the color of fire?
Is the color of blood the color of fire?
Is the red on the flag the color of fate?
Is the fate of our race the color of blood?
Is the color of fate the color of fire?
What is the fate of the blood of our race?
Strawberry jam?

To Restrict Freedom

Dumb
Freedom
Strict freedom
Restrict freedom
To restrict freedom
Wrong to restrict freedom
Not wrong to restrict freedom
It's not wrong to restrict freedom
It's not wrong to restrict freedom if
It's not wrong to restrict freedom if it
It's not wrong to restrict freedom if it is
It's not wrong to restrict freedom if it is necessary
It's not wrong to restrict freedom if it is necessary to
It's not wrong to restrict freedom if it is necessary to keep
It's not wrong to restrict freedom if it is necessary to keep people
It's not wrong to restrict freedom if it is necessary to keep people safe
I
It
Hit
Shit
Bullshit.

Rhythm Method

rhythm method   a method of seeking birth
control
by abstaining
from sexual intercourse
during a woman's (probable) monthly

v
u
l
a
t
i
o
n

period

The Greatest Hits of Neptoon Rising

The calf is newly born now:
This Wildebeest is Gnu.
Wind blue in sky,
The clouds are dry—
They don't know what to dew.

When cell does cell division,
It multiplies, it's true;
The daughter cell
Then starts to swell,
Then daughter's splittin' too.

I'm hungry at the track field,
I cannot eat the meet;
Still I'll be fed
A food that's red,
When one team there is beat.

The beast is very grizzly,
It's more than I can bear.
And are the ants
Still in my pants:
There, over, under, where?

The bee is on a string that
Is knotted in the sea.
I can't decide
If sea is tide
To bee or knot to bee.

So John, sew Paul and Ringo,
Sea hare is on your head;
Your voice regrets
Your guitar's frets.
Eye seize your book, it's red.

Thank ewe.

Sleepwalk or Something

The seal was stamped on the stately sheet,
Seal swam the sea through snow and sleet,
Slow and slim, through slime swam she,
Sealed the fate of the Holy See;
The seal sealed by Sal on ceiling sits still.
The still still sits on the silly sill.
The shoeless sow near the sill saw sod,
Where a sow with shoes slobbered on scrod;
The shod sow in sod said to scrod, so shy,
"Why shoe a sow? One should shoo a fly."
A Swami swam, saw seamen seemin' snide,
In a scull with a skull on its starboard side.
The seamen on the stern were stern; they'd swear
They'd sneeze when they'd seize the seas in their snare.
Swami said to seamen, every Tao and Zen,
"Seine the Seine for salmon, with Sam on fen."
One seaman shot semen, saw no salmon, then,
With no salmon seen, insane to seine Seine.
Sad Stu, in a stew, whose suit was shred,
Had head swelled swell by something said:
The needle said thread, or sew it seamed.
Sad Stu's soft stew seemed swiftly steamed.
Cy's suit size seemed six too small,
So Cy sighed a sigh on side of stall.
Some sea side girls' swim suits at shore
Let Seymore see more flesh for sure.
The heath was small as sin at shore:
Seymore could see a little moor.
Sey saw a saw from Arkansas;
Seasaw went the sea, the sea Sey saw.
Cy saw the saw (the saw Sey saw),
So Cy and Sey sawed salvaged straw.

(They would have sawed wood, not saffron straw,
But wood would never rhyme with saw).
Sam set to set the set to a sum,
But some of the sum seemed sort of dumb,
So he summoned some to sum and come,
And some to sum the sum of some.
With some too sick to seek his schtick,
Sam sicked the sick "a pun Sikh" (sic).
The squaw's son squawked, sat in soft sun.
"The squid squeezed squab"—squib should stun.
The sun set saffron on sandalwood;
The stars shined of satin, where Satan stood.
The siren casts spells, but spells itt wrong,
The fire engine sings the siren's song.
The saints summoned Solomon, and stayed for stew;
Stu did stew, stopped to Solomon sue;
Sue sat sadly and sheared the sheep;
She saw such silliness, she sank to sleep.
Stu sacked his suit, in the sack it fit.
Stu sought a loo in a shack, to sit.
Lou severed silence, stood to stroll.
My shoe sheltered sweat, upon my sole–
My sole sole for supper, near Stu's suit stoop.
Sue shouted, "I scream," and got the scoop.
She scooped six cents with good sense too,
Went sailing, in saline, the ocean blue,
Took stock of her stock from where she sat.
The sinner man sought cinnamon, or something like that.

Poem Without End

This is a poem with no ending;
Its next line's forever pending;
One day I started writing it thinking I'm a whiz;
You'll never finish reading it, and the reason is
This is a poem with no ending;
Its next line's forever pending;
One day I started writing it thinking I'm a whiz;
You'll never finish reading it, and the reason is
This is a poem with no ending;
Its next line's forever pending;
One day I started writing it thinking I'm a whiz;
You'll never finish reading it, and the reason is
Etc.

AUTHOR'S COMMENTARY
ON THE POEMS

Midnight

Alliteration, rhythm, and rhyme re-enforce the feeling. This poem reveals a unity among love of nature, romantic love, and erotic love. This is a multidimensional poem, in that eroticism underlies the theme on the surface, which of course is romantic love; many double meanings are used to accomplish this. There is an interesting and beautiful contrast in lines 3 and 4 when the speaker says,

> "We'll be white in the candle of moonlight,
> We'll be black in the ocean's red roar."

Sinner's Rue

Imagery, rhythm, rhyme, and alliteration re-enforce the story. Look for specific examples of each of these.

There is a pun in line 1 of stanza 7: "Mocker" is short for Mockingbird, and represents the forces of nature that mock Janet, which collectively are a mocker. The word "false" has two meanings here as well, although I would not call it a pun. The song of the Mockingbird is "false", because in real life, this bird sings the songs of many other bird species, skillfully mimicking them. Also, the Mocker is false because it is symbolic of and is personified by Thomas and Janet, and their deceitfulness. There is another pun in line 1 of stanza 9: Thomas' "seedy lover" is seedy because of her seeds in her necklace, and because of her dishonest nature.

They bury Janet:

> "By some flowers too faded for lovers,
> By a creek that was too dry to sing."

This is poignantly symbolic of their nature, what they did to Janet, and the poem's story.

Stanza 16 breaks the serious drama of the poem with humor in its first line ("All over the granite and Janet").

Stanza 18 states some beautiful moral philosophy:

> "Walk on the lighted path, always;
> To yourself and the world, remain true."

I liked these lines so much that I listed them at the beginning of this book as a quote of the author.

There is irony in how Thomas keeps his promise in the twist ending. I will not explain why Sinner's Rue grew at Janet's gravesite (and hence allowed Thomas to catch his foot in it, get his head smashed, and involuntarily keep part of his promise to Janet). That is for the reader to figure out; it can be found with a careful reading of the poem. The discovery of this by the reader should be satisfying, and makes for an interesting facet of this poem. "Nobody knew why it grew there." But the observant reader knows.

For You

In line 1, mist sounds like midst—a play on words. There is an unusual rhyme of "sunset" and "done yet". There is original language in "sky that is changing its blue" and in the last line. The simplicity and unique, original language result in surprises.

You

Enjoy the images and colors; spin at the speed of night.

As Bondage Ever Freedom Seeks

There is a pun on the word "partial", and it is used with a line break, resulting in a different meaning if line 10 is read alone than if read together with line 11. Line 12 also has a slightly different meaning if the line is read alone as opposed to being read with the two lines following it.

Love Lies Still

The first words of lines 3 and 4 of stanza 1 rhyme with each other; likewise for stanza 3.

In stanza 2, the word "light" in line 3 is a pun with three meanings: light from the sun, (the wing is) not heavy, and to land on something. Line 4 of this stanza and line 3 of stanza 3 have two-letter alliterations (using the letters "fl").

In stanza 3, flocks and phlox are homonyms, so these words at the end of lines make what is called a near rhyme, or half rhyme. The words "flight" and "white" in front of them make them into the two-word phrases "flight flocks" and "white phlox" that are full rhymes at the end of the lines. The three-word alliteration in line 3 of the stanza and the novelty given by the very different spellings of "flocks" and "phlox," together with these near and full rhymes, makes for an interesting stanza.

In the last line of the poem, the jarring switching of the words "lies" and "still," with the pun, adds emotional punch and shock, and creates a surprise ending.

Succession

The plants mentioned indicate the site of this poem is likely somewhere in California. All of the plants in the poem occur together in some parts of this state.

The name of this poem, "Succession", has a double meaning. There is a succession of lovers replacing one another. This is paralleled with references to ecological succession, a common phenomenon in nature in which plant communities replace each other successively, generally in order of increasing complexity. The plant communities in the poem are mentioned in the same sequence as ecological succession actually takes place within botanical communities in nature: lichens are first; they are replaced by small plants, such as clover; this is replaced by more complex plant communities, in this poem consisting of poppies and rye; lastly, there appears the final community of trees, which are oaks in the poem. Full disclosure dictates that I tell you that only some of the many species of clover in California appear before and are eventually shaded out by rye, and hence are a stage in succession prior to it. And poppies overlap in time of appearance with clover so much that they might not fully qualify as a later successional stage than any California clover species, although there may be one or two that this is true for. Of course, it only takes one clover species that qualifies as an earlier stage in succession than both rye and poppies for the poem to be scientifically valid, so the poem almost certainly is. If not, I think a little poetic license is permissible here.

Of course, the orange and amber are the colors of the poppies and rye. The poppies have to be California Poppies, since this species is orange. Opium is made from a different species of poppy than the California Poppy, but this point is not relevant to symbolism. Thus, you could view the poppy fields in this poem as a symbol of your choosing, since the Opium Poppy induces a dream-like sleep and altered states of consciousness.

This poem has a rhythm of people walking, adding to its emotion and giving its rhythm unity with its described action, because this is what the lovers do in the fields of orange and amber. A good deal of alliteration and, in line 8, assonance, re-enforce the poem's meaning and feeling.

An ironic twist ends the first stanza. The term "climax pair" in the second-to-last line referring to the couple goes with the scientific term for the final plant community in ecological succession—the climax community. This is oaks in the poem. Although "climax" has the double meaning of referring to both the couple and the oak community as the final state, there is no intended sexual meaning in the word in this poem.

Eyes of Chocolate

Chocolate eyes can be symbolic for any darker skin color or race, and even go beyond that to symbolize anything different—an adventure or different path in life.

In stanza 2, lines 19 and 20, there are puns on three different words for deer (fawn, deer, hart):

> "And fawn on me, my chocolate tart,
> She'd be my deer, I her sweet hart."

I'm surprised no poet has discovered this before, given the long history of poetry, but I am not aware of any poem that employs this group of three puns together. Therefore, as far as I know, I am the first to do so in a poem.

Stanza 2, lines 29 and 30 say that

> "The camouflage of chocolate highs
> Helped chocolate lips hide chocolate lies."

The word "camouflage" refers to the fact that the highs made the lies metaphorically appear the same "color" as the truth.

There are a number of succinct, poetic, philosophical statements of wisdom, such as:

> "Yet when we choose a course or deed,
> We never know where it will lead,
> And speculating, 'What if, then?'
> Has never righted wrongs of men.
> Whatever plan, however great,
> Is subject to the whims of fate."

> "Blind reason, though, can spawn a mess"

> "To blind luck, our faults, or fate,
> Or to our mind's demanding state,
> Each of us is but a slave".

Although I would never attempt to claim I am comparable to him, succinct, poetic, philosophical statements of wisdom are one of the many aspects of Shakespeare's writing that I love.

In the Glen

Notice how the rhyme scheme and rhythm re-enforce the story and ending, and affect you.

In the last line of the stanza 3, there is a pun on the word "hear", since it could read, "Here joy and love will stay", though this reading requires the elimination of the comma after the word "joy".

There is a pun on the word "sound" in stanza 8: "Our sleep would thus be sound."

The last stanza does not overtly state it, and it is subtle, but one can infer from this stanza that the speaker's lover died, giving a surprising, twist ending to the poem. Note the speaker's sudden change in his attitude toward the birds and their songs. Alliteration and soft sounds ("cease your senseless") together with hard sounds, such as "clatter" and "chatter", add to the startling, powerful effect of the ending.

Beckoneeng Hill

Apparently talking about the flowers, the speaker is really talking about his deceased love, Molly Brown. The names and descriptions of the flowers have double meanings, referring not only to flowers, but also to Molly Brown and her untimely death. The line, "Blue dyes my heart from the cast of the die" puns several times. "Blue dyes my heart" has two meanings: the color blue dyes my heart; and "Blue dies my heart" has an inversion of words, meaning my heart dies with a blue color (sadly). Also, the word "blue" refers back to the color of the flower referred to at the stanza's beginning, the Bluebonnet. "Cast of the die" has several meanings: roll of one die; shade (cast) of one die rolled; shade (cast) of the dye; a throwing *or* shade (two separate meanings of cast) of dying, "the die" referring to the speaker's dying. Each of the two meanings of "blue dyes my heart" can be put together with each of the various meanings of "the cast of the die" to yield several different combinations, each with its own unique meaning, for several different meanings of the line. The last stanza shocks when it tells us that the speaker intends to commit suicide to join his love, as he intends to "push up the flowers of Beckoneeng Hill".

The plants in this poem would not all grow together in the wild, so this poem refers to a cultivated garden. These plants could all grow together in a garden in some areas, such as parts of California, where I fancy the poem takes place. Some of the species do differ from some of the others in their requirements for moisture, sun, and other needs, but a skilled, motivated gardener could get them all to grow together, and get each of them to persist for several years, by catering to the needs of each species. The common names for many refer to many possible different species. All have at least one species that a gardener might want to grow, except hemlock, which could easily grow in or close to the garden as an unplanted weed in California; this is certainly true of Poison Hemlock, introduced to California from Greece, and the deadly plant that was used to poison Socrates. This is the hemlock of this poem. Most or even all of the species could possibly be made to bloom at the same time of the year with proper cultivation, but this would not be necessary to make the poem botanically correct, since the speaker is not necessarily saying all the plants are flowering and sending the messages he fancies they are sending as he speaks, but possibly at various times of the year. The Foxtail sets seeds in spring when the Bleeding-heart is in flower, so its seeds could pierce this flower, as described in the poem.

Technically, one does not capitalize the name of an organism unless it represents a particular species or subspecies. For example, since there are several species of bleeding-heart, one would not generally capitalize it unless one was referring to a particular species, such as Luzon Bleeding-heart. However, since this piece is a poem, since it features plants and flowers, and for the sake of consistency, I capitalized all flowers and plants mentioned.

Velvet Blue

Note the use of repetition of the words "velvet blue". Stanzas 6 and 7 list the colors of a rainbow in the order they appear in nature, ending with the blue of the grieving woman's velvet blue. Hence, the poem is correct in stating that she "completes the rainbow".

The last stanza surprises when it reveals the relationship of the speaker to the subject of the poem. In the last stanza, the speaker is revealed to be so in love with the poem's subject that he'll wait a lifetime for her. Also, up until the last stanza, the speaker was the narrator of the poem, telling the woman's story. The last stanza adds to the surprise when the speaker changes from speaking about the subject of the poem to speaking to her.

As to the poem's scientific accuracy, the Northern Cardinal, Evening Grosbeak, and Canadian Yew could occur together in autumn in a northeastern U. S. forest with deciduous trees, which would tend to display some bright orange leaves at that time of year.

My Only Song

Note that the speaker of a poem is the one narrating the poem, and is not necessarily the author, although the speaker is sometimes the author. Let me assure the reader that in this case, the speaker is not the author. There is lively, original language in parts, such as "It melts my blue to green" and "peace steams through my spleen." This poem has a twist ending that is a shocker and a surprise. And a careful reading will reveal that there is nothing inconsistent in the speaker's character as painted in the poem with the shocking action at its end.

Springtime

The reader expects a romantic ending to this verse, since it seems to be building up to it. But it doesn't happen. The simplicity, simple rhythm, and seeming predictability of this poem make its surprise, unpredictable, twist ending more poignant.

Loving Words Are Flowers

This poem has many puns and plays on words linking plants and flowers to human body parts, as it uses metaphors of humans and their loving words as plants and flowers. The words "leaves" (line 5), "stems" (line 6), and "petals" (line 8) are puns or plays on words that are used as both verbs and nouns. In the case of the word "petals", the verb is another, but similar-sounding, word: "pedals". Other cases in which a double meaning is achieved through words that sound like other words are: "pouring brain" sounds like "pouring rain", and "human soil" sounds like "human soul".

There's Nothing You Can Do That Can't Be Done

The poem makes the point that love greatly nurtures the giver of love, not just its recipient, without saying it, but by asking a question. I hoped this achieved subtlety in delivering this message. The title is appropriately a line from the Beatles' song, "All You Need Is Love".

When the Woodlark Sings Deep in the Heather

Stanza 3 has a pun on "whether", and an internal rhyme ("heather "in line 2 rhymes with the last words of lines 1 and 3).

In stanza 4, the spring came "in plastic and leather" because it was full of the artificial things made by humans. This stanza's last line has the pun: "Would larks…" (Woodlarks). This line has yet another, more subtle meaning, a secondary pun, which requires imagining the question mark removed: I wish jokes played on my heart would fly (away).

There is a surprise ending: the couple is not together in the heather, not because of breaking up, as the speaker feared might happen, but because of destruction of the heather. Of course, the poem has an environmental theme.

The Woodlark (*Lullula arborea*) is known for its beautiful song; in fact, its generic name *Lullula* derives from its sweet plaintive song, delivered in flight from heights of 300 feet or more. But it does breed in heather as well as other habitats, and will sing in heather. Besides, flying well above the heather in song, as it will do, could be considered singing in the heather, in that it is in the habitat of heather. It breeds across most of Europe, including Great Britain; the Middle East; Asia; and the mountains of north Africa. It is mainly brown above, consistent with the poem's reference to "a brown Woodlark" and "tan-feathered tears".

Never Cry

This poem never uses the word "wolf" until its very last word, even though the wolf is its subject. Even the title leaves out the word "wolf", even as it refers to the expression, "Never cry wolf". In the second stanza, there are four times when quotation marks appear around four blank spaces (for the four letters in the word "wolf), allowing the reader to fill in the word "wolf". The poem makes many references to the wolf.

"Schemes to suck on her Romulus-and-Remus-like" refers to Romulus and Remus, who, according to legend, were twin brothers who were suckled by a female wolf as babies. Later, says the legend, Romulus killed Remus, then founded Rome, and was its first king.

Consider stanza 4 of the poem, which says:

> "My wish for your race
> is a
> *backward spell*
> of the
> *evil flow*
> of progress!"

Backward spell is a pun. The two meanings are as follows. The speaker wishes a spell to be cast on the evil, destructive flow of human progress, and the speaker wishes for the wolf the meaning of the words "evil flow" spelled backward. "Evil flow" spelled backward is "wolf live"!

The last two lines,

> "I'll have to be
> as gentle as a wolf,"

are very powerful in that wolves are not thought of as gentle, but in reality are social animals that are normally gentle. Also, the last word of the poem is the only time that the word "wolf" is used in the poem.

I wrote two versions of "Never Cry". The two versions differ only in three lines (the third to fifth lines of the second stanza). The version in The Poems section of this book is the original version that I consider the real version; it is more poetic, but suitable only to mature readers. I call this the official version. In the other version, I re-wrote the three lines that are for mature audiences only in a form which is suitable for people of all ages. I call this the family version. I wrote the family version so that the institutions I donated the poem to or submitted it to for publication in their newsletter or other publication could choose the version they want, according to whether they intend to display the poem in a setting where children would view it or not; hence, they have a choice between a more poetic version and one safe from offending the sensitive reader. The family version of the poem, followed by both versions of the three lines that differ from each other in the two versions of the poem, appears immediately below this discussion.

I donated this poem to Wolf Haven International, in Tenino, Washington. This organization is dedicated to wolf conservation through educating the general public, and it has exhibits of live wolves. They have this poem with my biography accompanying it prominently displayed on beautiful parchment in their gift shop. They are displaying the family version. The official version of this poem was published in two newsletters. One is Volume 10, Issue 1 (Spring, 2007 issue) of *Restoring Connections*, the newsletter of the Sky Island Alliance, which is based in Tucson, Arizona. Each issue of their newsletter has a theme, and this issue's theme is geology. It has other poetry in it. The Sky Island Alliance is an organization dedicated to the preservation and restoration of native biological diversity in the sky islands of the southwestern U. S. and northwestern Mexico. A sky island is a mountain range isolated from other mountain ranges. The ones they work to preserve have exceptionally high biological diversity. The other place that "Never Cry" was published is the Spring/Summer, 2007 issue of *Arizona Wild*, the newsletter of the Arizona Wilderness Coalition, which has its main office in Tucson, Arizona, and works to permanently protect and restore wilderness and other wild lands and waters in Arizona. They are publishing it next to an article about wolves. My poem's publication in *Arizona Wild* is the first time this journal has ever published an artistic piece of any kind, and is likely starting a trend, since their editorial staff has indicated they will probably now start publishing such pieces in future issues of their newsletter.

Never Cry (Family Version)

Your eyes, still shining mustard-moon yellow,
still able to awaken the walking dead,
are going out like two candles

melting their last bits of wax;
a bullet hole in your head
as wide as a dry desert river bed;
your head in my arms;
and a gun,
smoking like an extinguished campfire,
carried away by a running
marksman, manicured and masculine in his cowboy boots,
with bloody hands,
and an excuse of one dead sheep
(killed by disease).

Scapedog, we project our nature onto you,
create myths that misrepresent you:
when a man chases a green young woman,
with schemes to feed on her
as Romulus and Remus did,
thoughtless of love,
we raise our snouts,
dangle our tongues,
and howl, "   !"
When we tell our children fairy tales
of villainous, deceitful
predators of hairy-chinned little piggies,
grandmothers, and
little girls, red and innocent in their riding hoods,
we lick our chops,
bear our teeth,
and huff and puff, "   !"
When our sheep and cattle die
from brutal conditions leaving
stress, starvation, and disease in their wake,
or when buffalo, elk, deer, antelope disappear
in silver gun smoke,
we lower our heads,
raise our lips,
and growl, "   !"

When someone sucks
food straight into the stomach
like a vacuum cleaner
at relativistic speed,
we chomp on our teeth,
swallow our saliva,
and yelp that this is to "   " it down.
Without predators to offer us the possibility of death,
without the primal howl of evolution's night,
where is the wild in wilderness?
How will we awaken to our nature's connection to nature?
Or to the strands of spider-silk that tether us to the Universe?
Domesticated dogs can't awaken domesticated minds.

My wish for your race
is a
backward spell
on the
evil flow
of progress!

I could tear flesh,
rage like a mad dog
in anger about this bloody killing,
and howl madly
at the moon
about the need
to protect your species.
But that would be
taken as another excuse to kill
your brothers and sisters.
No: to defend your race,
I'll have to be
as gentle as a wolf.

Three Lines That Differ Between Official And Family Versions

Official Version

when a man comes salivating on a virgin's breasts,
with schemes to suck on her Romulus-and-Remus-like,
and penetrate her,

Family Version

when a man chases a green young woman,
with schemes to feed on her
as Romulus and Remus did,

Another Song

This poem's title, "Another Song", can be viewed as another song has come because the cicadas sing alone at a different time of year and from a different place, or that there will be another song after humans drive themselves extinct and new species of animals evolve and sing with cicadas, which would at that point once again sing in their natural location and time of year. This poem speaks a good deal about song, so, true to my belief that the form of a poem should fit and re-enforce its subject and meaning, it has musical alliterations, assonances, and internal rhymes. For example, consider these alliterations in the first line: "Cicadas are silent in summer." This line has the hard "c" and "d" for harsh sounds (cacophony), and the soft "c", and the "s" three times, for soft sounds (harmony), so the line intersperses cacophony with harmony.

Cicadas are insects that live as larval forms from several months to many years underground (depending on the species), then emerge as adults to live and mate for only a number of weeks in spring and/or summer (also depending on the species). The males sing in the trees to attract females to mate with them. There is a curse in Greek literature that says, "Your cicalas shall sing from the ground." Cicala is a poetic form of cicada. Since adult cicadas live in trees, the curse is wishing the loss of trees on its recipient. The line in this poem, "And now they sing from the ground" similarly refers to forests having been cut down by humans.

The last line of stanza 5, in saying that the sunlight is red at midday, is ominous, and this may be interpreted in more than one way. It is a good exercise for the reader to play with different interpretations of this line.

All nature is painted as being interrelated, and even song is included as being unified with life and nature. Thus, when humans destroy the other singers than the cicadas, the cicadas lose their connection with other singing species, and so sing, "Alone, so way out of tune".

Gaian Slumber

This poem has interesting internal rhymes and near rhymes, and an effective rhyme of the line ending with "mirth" with the last line, ending in "earth!" Notice the imagery; for example, "Terse virgin indigo and urgent white" and "fluorescent ocelots".

All of the earth queen's body parts are, or are associated with, living things in nature, except one. The exception: the "eyes of molten emerald", in stanza 1, line 4, which are green like nature, since emerald is green, and valuable like nature, because emerald is a precious gem. But it is the eyes that we see with, and emerald is a hard, inanimate substance, consistent with the fact that she is frozen and unable to see or act, since she is unaware of what is going on, being asleep. Her eyes are "molten" emerald because she has the passion to want to stop the destruction of the earth, if she were aware of it.

The sea is "bitter" (stanza 1, line 7) because of the destruction of nature, and lack of awareness and action to rectify this destruction.

The queen can symbolize Mother Nature, but, since she is asleep in a blissful dream, she can also signify the lack of awareness of much of the human race to the fact that it is destroying the earth and its life.

Gold

There is poetic repetition of the word "gold". Gold has the symbolic representation of the beauty of nature, and beauty and joy of life, in addition to its literal meaning.

Line 4 has a triple meaning for "golden mean". On the color chart, and on the spectrum of the colors of white light separated into its component colors by a prism, yellow (gold) is between orange and green, adjacent to and equidistant from each of them. Hence orange and green sum to a golden mean (average). Secondly, the golden mean is a happy medium between two extremes. Finally, the golden mean is a ratio that occurs in a mathematical set of numbers known as the Fibonocci series. The ancient Greeks considered a rectangle with its sides in this ratio to be especially pleasing to the eye, and built such buildings as the Parthenon using this ratio for its sides. Leonardo da Vinci considered the golden mean the perfect ratio for certain proportions in the human body. It is very important in mathematics. It occurs repeatedly in nature; for example, the placement of petals on some species of flowers and of leaves on some species of plants, and the rate of spiraling of some snail shells and galaxies are represented by the golden mean. Note the internal rhyme in this fourth line: "come to a sum".

Lines 16 and 17 refer the poem "Nothing Gold Can Stay", by Robert Frost, with a pun on Frost's name.

Earth Drums

The rhythm of the first two lines, with help from line breaks, is a rhythm similar to petals dancing back and forth in the wind. The last two lines, with the alliteration of "d" sounds in "drop" and "drumbeats", and with all words being one syllable except one (which is of only two syllables), sounds like water dripping off the petals and hitting the ground.

Tears of Ecstasy

There is lovely assonance in: "Since streams seethe with steam deep in pollywog bogs". There are lively, fresh adjectives in: "For star-dappled sea slugs, for plum-brindled sky". There is a pun in "Green ecstasy's tears are filling my I". Alliteration re-enforces and harmonizes with the sentiment of the poem. This is a celebration of nature's profound beauty.

Dawn

There is beauty in nature, particularly in the transition from night to day called dawn. There is profound sadness that dawn must disappear. Yet, because dawn is forever appearing in a spot on earth just beyond where it just faded, and because dawn always exists somewhere on earth, dawn never dies, even though, seemingly paradoxically, it is always dying. The rotation of the earth plays a big role in causing this, and like the earth's rotation, the constant death and paradoxical eternity of dawn is a circular, cyclic phenomenon. This theme of circular continuity is re-enforced in the poem by the fact that the first word of many lines sounds identical to or very similar to the last word of the previous line, but with a different meaning.

Stanza 1 is technically not a complete sentence, and adding the word "is" to lines 1 and 3 would make it so. "Is," the third person of the verb "to be," is implied without being stated. The significance of this is that the poem is about dawn's continuing death and existence—that is, whether dawn *is*.

I think stanza 3 is beautiful and interesting.

For this poem to be scientifically correct, the thrasher would most likely be a Sage Thrasher, which breeds in sagebrush habitats in the western U. S., and the eagle a Golden Eagle, which can occur in this geographic area and these habitats. I imagine a wide area with the downs with bees and flowers, the forest, and the mountains mentioned in the poem all in close proximity to each other and the sagebrush habitat. This is possible in some areas in the western U. S.

The Glimpse

Venus is the Roman goddess of love, Mars the Roman god of war. Think of the many meanings and connotations of "green" and "red", which I used to modify Venus and Mars, respectively. (By the way, the planet Mars is actually red). The line, "Fresh with lust, as newly wed" is interesting because marriage is generally associated with other attributes than lust, yet newly weds do tend to lust for each other. Truth, claims the poem, is "partly substance, partly dreams". Hence, the poem argues that one must use one's imagination, as well as recognize physical reality, to arrive at truth.

Affirmation

The line break after the line, "I fancy the world" (line 14), causes the line taken alone to have a very different meaning from the line taken with the lines following it:

> "I fancy the world
> expresses its piercing
> pain in the wolf's howl..."

In an otherwise unrhymed poem, the last two lines rhyme, to make an effective, surprise ending, as nature answers the question of the speaker, changing the poem from one of despair to a positive outlook and appreciation of the beauty of nature and reality.

Metamorphosis

Enjoy the internal rhymes, and the many–often play-ful–words with similar sounds within the same line; for example, "I'd see me so seamy I'd die." There are interesting references to Australia's wildlife and Aboriginal culture, and multiple meanings of words for colors.

The speaker undergoes a transformation of consciousness that leads to the unexpected last line and surprise ending, and accounts for the title. Someone who read this poem told me that the speaker referring to his Aboriginal guide as "primitive you" gives a condescending, colonial feel to the poem. Of course, it does not, for he missed the point: the phrase serves to tell the reader the mindset of the frightened, narrow-minded speaker, with his parochial outlook, before he under-went his metamorphosis to a more enlightened state.

Transcendence

Several references to white, snow, and the Snowy Owl make them symbols, and gives them many meanings, such as consciousness. Think of others yourself. The form of the poem matches its meaning. As the speaker sinks into his compulsive need to label the owl, the poem transforms from one of rhyme and rhythm to one of free form, with no rhyme or recurring rhythm. When the speaker is in a more relaxed, spiritual state that transcends the need for labels and words, which occurs both before and after the speaker falls out of this state and into the compulsive labeling mindset, the poem is rhymed and rhythmic, with its simple, short, four-syllable lines.

Snowy Owls live in the Arctic tundra and open grasslands, and only rarely venture into forested areas. So while they would only rarely be perched in a tree in the woods, they can be seen doing this occasionally.

Once upon a Cloudless Sulphur

"Once upon a Cloudless Sulphur" makes an analogy of metamorphosis in the lepidoptera (butterflies and moths) to human spiritual transformation, and this analogy and the transformation are the themes of the poem. Both the lepidopteran and the human require death to give birth to something new, and, at least in a sense, better. In the lepidopterans, of course, the caterpillar must "die" to transform into a beautiful, winged adult butterfly or moth, while in the human, the ego, lower self, or childish one must die to allow the birth and emergence of the fully developed, mature, spiritual, higher self. Both involve transformation.

Note the pun on Golden Fleece. I love stanza 6. Skipper is a play on words because it is also a butterfly species. The third eye, also known as the inner eye, is thought of as the gate that leads within to inner realms of higher consciousness. Polyphemus was a giant Cyclops in the *Odyssey* by the Greek poet, Homer; it is also a large moth that has large false eye-spots on its wings to scare off predators. The analogy with a Cyclops is apt because its sole eye is at least approximately in the same place as the third eye. In stanzas 7 and 8, I refer to the resemblance of the sarcophagi of ancient Egypt to Spinx Moth chrysalids, with a play on words between the Sphinx Moth and the Egyptian sphinx, and analogize the wrapped mummy to a cocoon as a larva in its wrapping. In fact, there is no evidence that the ancient Egyptians intentionally built their sarcophagi to resemble Sphinx Moth chrysalids, thought of transformation after death as analogous to the metamorphosis of a caterpillar into a Sphinx Moth or other lepidopteran, fancied mummies as cocoons, or had as part of their theology the idea of transformation after death into a sphinx. Also, the sarcophagus was not thought to carry the deceased into the sky. Entities roughly analogous to our soul were believed to go to the sky without the sarcophagus. So this is a leap of imagination, and a rare apparent violation of my principle that poems should be true to science and reality. However, I intend this to be read metaphorically and not literally, so I do not think it is a violation of the principle in actuality. And it is interesting to note that, although the ancient Egyptians did not intend it, the curled beard on the sarcophagi and coffins of pharaohs and some people who were not royalty resembled the proboscis (tongue) of adult lepidopterins in that it was curled, although in the opposite direction as that of the insect's tongue. And the ancient Egyptians did indeed believe that their pharaohs (and, in the New Kingdom, some who were not royalty) sailed in a boat in the sky after death to a new life in the celestial realm. I think that the comparison of the cocoon to a mummy in stanza 8 is interesting.

The following words have double meanings, with one meaning being the common name of a butterfly or moth, accounting for why I capitalized the words: Skipper, Polyphemus, Sphinxes, Elfin, Monarch, Lady, Nymph, Admiral, Swallow tales (the butterflies are Swallowtails in this play on words), Rambler, Satyr, Hermits, Mourning Cloak, Cloudless Sulphur, and Purplish Copper. In stanza 10, note that even hermits (or Hermits, in the meaning of the word that is a butterfly), who prefer to be alone, and hence unconnected to people, have to face that we are all connected by the need for a part of us (our ego, lower self) to die for inner transformation, so we all must wear a morning cloak (capitalized in poem, since it is also a butterfly species) in mourning for this death, since part of us does not want it to die, even though its death leads to our inner growth.

Technically, most of the common names should not be capitalized, since this is only conventionally done when one refers to the specific species, as in the Mourning Cloak butterfly, and not when one refers to a general group like the satyrs (which include, for example the Pine Satyr and the Red Satyr), but this convention is not always strictly followed, and I used my poetic license to capitalize all common names of butterflies and moths to emphasize their meaning as lepidopterans (which, of course, is in addition to the other meaning of these words as used in the verse).

By the way, although the preferred American spelling of the element is sulfur, with the variant, now especially British, spelling being sulphur, the butterfly is spelled "Cloudless Sulphur".

I have not discussed some of the most delightful alliterations, assonances, rhymes, sound repetitions, and other interesting aspects of this poem in this discussion, for I have decided to let the readers discover them for themselves, but do study especially stanzas 1 to 4, 7, 10, 13, and 14. However, do not limit yourself to these stanzas in enjoying delightful sound devices in this poem.

Reflections of Moondrops on Whispering Lake

In line 11 is a pun on the word "lie". Line 14: The Greek philosopher Plato, in his famous allegory of the cave, said people untutored in his Theory of Forms are like prisoners chained in a cave, unable to turn their heads, only able to see the cave's wall. A fire burns behind them, and between the fire and the prisoner's back, puppeteers hold up puppets that cast shadows on the cave's wall that the prisoners can see. The prisoners are unable to see the puppets, which are the real objects. The prisoners would think the shadows are real, mistaking appearance for reality, knowing nothing of the real cause of the shadows.

Follow the Light and Where

There a pun on the words "where/ wear". "Where" is used in a novel, unusual way, with a new meaning or set of meanings. In this poem, it is even used as parts of speech for which it is not normally used. Usually it is used as an adverb or a conjunction, less often as a pronoun, and occasionally as a noun (tell me the when and *where* of the wedding), but generally not more than one of these at once. In this poem, it is easy to interpret it as a noun, but in a somewhat different way than conventionally used: "Follow the...where", or, "Follow the light and (the) where". But it could be interpreted as any of the eight parts of speech in this poem, although for some parts of speech, one would have to imagine at least one word after it. It is a useful exercise to imagine how one could interpret the word "where" as each of the eight parts of speech in this poem. "Follow the light" could mean be loving and compassionate, seek wisdom, or follow the path to enlightenment, while "follow the where" might mean follow the unknown, follow the mystery. "Follow the light and where" might then be any combination of these meanings. However, I want to emphasize the importance of my intent to allow the reader to make his or her own interpretation of the word "where" and the phrase "Follow the light and where", for there is no correct interpretation, and interpretation of these meanings is up to each individual.

Each stanza contains three lines that begin with words with the same sound (they are homonyms in some cases), punning with each line. Stanza 3 uses beat/beet four times, once with it at the end of a line, as well as at the beginning. This is partly because I loved the sound of the line,

"beat of the shaman beat".

The poem is saying that all races of people were once indigenous cultures, close to nature, hunter-gatherers, with a shamanic world view; in basic ways, we were all once like the Indians of the rainforest who are still living with nature. The poem connects all cultures and all peoples in this sense. The mention of moccasins twice in the stanza 1 is meant to make such a connection of Whites with Indians, for although moccasins are well known as Indian footwear, it is likely early European hunter-gatherers wore moccasins or similar footwear.

In stanza 2, the line, "if you can see the trees for the forest" reverses a common phrase, pointing out that seeing the details may be important to seeing the whole, and the full picture could obscure itself by obscuring the details. This is a twist on how this is typically viewed.

Amarinth, mentioned in stanza 3, is still eaten as a minor grain today, but was eaten by the Aztec Indians of Mexico as one of their main staples. Also in this stanza, the beet and wheat originated as foods of Caucasians, while corn, squash, and amaranth were originated in the New World by Indians, so we have another link of these two peoples when the poem says to beat a path back to these foods,

"at first cultivation and before",

since these are times when these two peoples had the basic similarities mentioned in the first sentence of the previous paragraph. The rest of the stanza continues to make this link. Line 9, "when we antelope danced", could be interpreted as our ancestors doing a general nature dance or ritual. Also, pre-historic humans in Europe may have done dances that they created from their observations of antelope that one could call "antelope dances", although I am not sure, even after researching the matter, if they were in contact with any antelope species regularly enough for this. Indians of North America successfully danced to entice Pronghorn Antelope to catch them, although the Pronghorn is not a true antelope. The line could also refer to our pre-industrial ancestors of Africa adopting dances from the antelope they saw regularly, since all of us ultimately have an African genesis. The idea of our pre-industrial ancestors creating and doing dances based on their observations of antelope are speculative, but highly plausible, since such peoples often created and danced dances based on their observations of animals.

The line break causes the first line in the two lines below to have a different meaning, depending on whether it is read alone or with the line following it:

"(we hunted and gathered almost all of our history
into stories)".

153

Siddhartha Gautama

Siddhartha Gautama was the name of the person who became the Buddha. This poem has many puns and plays on words, with references to Buddhism.

For example, line 1 has the double meaning that he literally went out into the dark, or he went out like a light goes out. The latter meaning could refer to his starting out in an unenlightened state, or to his stopping his thoughts, which is a meditative state that aids on the road to awakening or enlightenment.

In line 2, "He lost himself found" refers to paradoxes in Eastern spirituality as one travels the road to enlightenment. Also, it may be viewed as follows: he had to lose himself in life and in the moment, by being fully present in it, and/or to lose his old habitual ways of thinking and his mental chatter, to find himself.

Line 4 says he "sat in a whole". This means he sat in an empty void; it also means he sat in the totality of things.

Line 4 then says that he sat "where his I's couldn't Rome". Hence, his eyes and his I's could not distract him from the goal of attaining higher states of consciousness. The eyes—both inner and outer—see, so it is important to keep them from roaming, and hence focused. "I's" refers to the many conflicting "I's", or parts, or inner voices, of a person that tend to fight for control with each other and with the higher self. "Rome" has a second meaning in keeping with the way I spelled it that symbolizes the material success and spiritual failure of an empire characterized by war, conquest, slavery, gladiator fights, material wealth, and so on. His eyes and I's could not roam to this Rome.

Line 5 leaves out the letter "e" wherever an apostrophe appears; hence the question of where did the "e" go, with the pun on the loss of his ego, a desired result of Buddhist practice. Also, "e" is the most common letter of the alphabet, so here represents verbal language and symbols, which, according to at least some schools of Buddhist thought, must be transcended in order to achieve enlightenment. "He was the tree grow" in line 5 equates him not only with the tree, a noun, but with the noun and verb together, "tree grow", meaning that the Buddha was indistinguishable from the tree, and even from the action the tree took, the verb "grow". This is saying that there is no border between things, and even things and actions; in other words, all is unified as one, a teaching of Buddhism and much Eastern philosophy. The words, "ask'd wh'r' did th' 'e' go?" leave out the pronoun "he" entirely, referring to his disappearance into the unity with all things, "The One", and to his transcendence and loss of self and his ego. This makes the pun on the loss of the ego especially appropriate here.

In addition to the more obvious meanings and pun in line 8, one can also view the owl, a nocturnal bird, as a creature of the night, and hence darkness and ignorance, and the diurnal lark as symbolizing the light of day, and hence enlightenment. Of course, this conflicts with the traditional view and symbolism of the owl as wise, which the line refers to.

In lines 9 and 10, the "el" sound is used three times: in "elephant", "elf", and "himself". This is of interest because in all Semitic languages—which include modern Arabic and Hebrew, and such ancient languages as Babylonian and Aramaic—what is pronounced "el" means a god, and, in some contexts, God. This is interesting for an additional reason: the area in the world where these languages are the primary languages is, of course, the historic center of Judaism, Christianity, and Islam; and Aramaic was the native tongue of Jesus Christ. Thus, there is also a geographic and historic link to religion, and hence to God. This subtle reference to God through Semitic languages has a relevance to the poem that supplements and strengthens it. This is especially powerful in the last line, since it both has one of these "el" sounds and mentions God, saying Siddhartha,

"Went looking for God, found only himself."

155

This final line says he found enlightenment, or "God", in himself, a major idea of at least some schools of Buddhist thought.

I hope this poem, with its simple couplets, brevity, plays on words, references to Buddhism and Eastern philosophy, and powerful form and message, stimulated the reader's inner growth.

Zen Meditation on the Nature of Reality

Having no words, this poem is as short as a poem can be. Thus, it holds the unbeatable world record as the shortest poem ever written. It also holds the unbeatable world record as the longest poem ever written, being without beginning or end, hence infinite in length. "Zen Meditation on the Nature of Reality" holds unbeatable world records as the shortest *and* the longest poem ever written. Think about it. Or, better yet, *don't* think about it.

The Way
to Shambhala

In Buddhist teaching, Shamabhala refers to an enlightened society or place of fearlessness, dignity, and compassion. It can refer to a literal place, often placed in central Asia; the mind and body; or meditative practice.

The title is in two lines in order that one line simply says "The Way".

What is the red wolf winter that the speaker tells us to come home to? Maybe

<blockquote>
"come home

to a red wolf winter"
</blockquote>

means face and experience the harsh side of life, including your dark side.

There is a near rhyme in lines 5 and 6 of "fear" and "mirror".

This Water

The history of one drop of water, listing some of the places where it has been, is used to convey this poem's message that all things are deeply, profoundly interrelated and interconnected. The last two lines, in taking the water from a Zen master's bucket to the black rain that fell on Hiroshima, starkly show the contradictions in the human race, and lend a startling ending.

Reel Whiz Dumb

Think about this poem on your own. Put in some effort. It should be well rewarded. It is generally more rewarding for you if you figure out poems and their wisdom on your own; this is especially true with this one.

As far as the line "Speak to the sage that the pine may hear" is concerned, sages and pine trees grow together in some places; for example, southern California. So the line is scientifically accurate.

Meditate, Tiger

This poem, like many literary works, can be interpreted in many ways, and no one interpretation is the "right" one. Likewise, the tiger in the poem can be correctly interpreted in many ways, with no one correct interpretation. That said, I think of the tiger as a person's higher self. Also, it could also be the will, or the creative force or muse of a person, or his or her intuition.

The many interesting, poetic lines in this work are not always immediately clear in meaning, but it is well worth the effort to comtemplate their meaning, and interpret them through a combination of both logic and intuition. My telling the meaning would be counter-productive, because the struggle to find the meaning is important to the reader's growth and understanding, my interpretation is not necessarily the correct one for reasons discussed above, and explaining a poem's meaning can take away from its power.

I especially love, and am particularly proud of, the lines,

> "a person could lose everything
> in the flap of a duck's wing."

Think about instances in your own life and in the lives of people you know that illustrate how frighteningly true this is.

Unreflecting Moon

The moon could be a symbol for our consciousness. I say "could be" because it could symbolize other things as well; that is for the reader to interpret.

The title is a pun: the literal moon cannot reflect light, and the moon as our consciousness cannot reflect (think).

In stanza 3, there is an interesting rhyme of "eclipse" with "ships". This stanza also has a pun in line 4: "As we fish and lose sight of the real". Here, "real" could also be spelled "reel", being a fishing reel.

Stanza 5 has an interesting rhyme of "seek" with "oblique".

Clay

Think about the meaning of the poem and why its last line says we are clay.

Do Due Duty

Yes, go, and do good. This poem is meant for more than the usual reasons to read poetry, such as enjoyment and pleasure; this poem is meant to inspire people spiritually and to inspire them to do good. I am not saying that no other poems do these things; I am saying that this poem aims for this more than most poems do.

The Key

No comments.

The Way They Look

No comments.

The Sky Was Silent and the Moon Was White

Stanza 1, line 3 says silence "named the name that can't be named." The *Tao Te Ching*, the famous book of wisdom by Lao Tzu, says the name that can be named is not the eternal Name. Did silence name the eternal Name, which we might consider the essence off reality?

I love stanza 1, line 11, "Washed in white and why."

Consider lines 12 to 22 of stanza 1. The Universe either ends with nothing beyond it, or goes on infinitely. Either way, it "stops at nothing," as the poem says. And in either case, we cannot understand or conceptualize it, because nothing and infinity are both concepts beyond our comprehension and imagination. So the Universe cannot be fully understood by humans.

In line 3 of stanza 2, "colorless white in all-colored light" has a physical reality in that white is the absence of color in material entities, such as paint, but in light, all colors together make white.

Of course, there is much more being said in the poem than this. It is best understood intuitively and through close attention and careful thought. Contemplate the poem and use your intuition as you read it again and again.

Mined

Although the line breaks hide it, there would be nine syllables in each line if the lines

> "Sea wind sea water sea waves sea
> Woe to the mind that can knot sea
> The flow..."

ended with the rhyming pair of words "woe" and "flow", thusly:

> "Sea wind sea water sea waves sea woe
> To the mind that can knot sea the flow."

Then, if we pick up at the lines:

> "Oh, wind oh to
> The inner dance that wakes me from
> My dreamy trance...,"

we would get eight syllables in the two lines that would end with the rhymed pair of words, this time "dance" and "trance". This continues in a consistent pattern, decreasing by one syllable each time, until we get two rhymed words that, if all lines ended in rhymed words, would be one-syllables lines:

> "Why
> I".

Also, each of these "couplets" with rhymes within lines and of decreasing numbers of syllables are separated from each other by two four-syllable lines that rhyme with each other, but, once again, with line breaks such that these four-syllable lines also do not yield rhymes at the end of lines. It's worth going over the poem and observing this if you are interested in this kind of novel line play. Because of what I just discussed, the line breaks are such that rhymed words do not generally occur at the end of lines, as is the case with most rhymed poems.

Note the puns and plays on words.

Waves and Tides

One interpretation of the symbols in this poem is that the waves and tides are the conscious mind, the wind is the drive for inner, spiritual (not necessarily religious) growth, and the moon is the unconscious mind. There may be other valid interpretations of this poem's symbolism.

Tell Me No Lies

The powerful rhythm and insistent character of the first five lines of each stanza strengthen the poem's theme, set a powerful tone, and make the poem forceful. Line 7 of each stanza is the last words of each of the six previous lines, in the same order as the lines appear. In line 8 of each stanza, the second through fifth words are the first words of the first four lines of the stanza, in the same order as the lines appear. The fourth word of line 6 of any given stanza rhymes with the fourth word of line 6 of all the other stanzas, and all of these fourth words are followed by either the words "is good" or "and good", making all of these sixth lines rhyme or near-rhyme with each other. Stanzas have interesting physical shapes. The rhythm and alliteration effectively support the poem's idea and power.

The Magpie

In this poem, the magpie is a metaphor for the man, who flew planes and flew to a high life. The three colors of the magpie's feathers are symbols for things that are spelled out by the magpies that discuss the man.

There are philosophical, poetic observations. For example,

"Men pray to God, but seek the meal".

There are metaphors. Two instances are:

"He played the magic fife,"

and

"What good are green, wealth, power, fame,
If one can't fly the kite?".

And there are plays on words; most notable of these to me is:

"He never saw the shades of jay,
Only black and spite,"

which substitutes for the well-known phrases "shades of gray" and "(seeing the world in) black and white". Another play on words is the pun:

"His game of life was never one
With the world, just fright."

Here, the word "one" can also be spelled "won".

At the end of the poem, the deceased man is

"A flightless magpie in a cage
Of green and black and white",

and has the three colors "in literal plight" because they
dressed him in a tuxedo (black and white), and he is wearing
grass (green), since he is under it. He does not have any of
the things that the three colors represent "except in literal
plight" because he is dead, so none of the three things they
symbolize can be in his possession.

Brief Is the Time

This poem is deceptively simple. It is brief, which is consistent with its theme of the brevity of beauty, precious phenomena, and life. It speaks of the brevity of all precious
things; indeed, of everything, of all existence. Alliteration, for
example in lines 1, 2, and 3, makes the point of the poem
more poignant.

There is a pun in the first line, which can also be read as
"Brief is the time that roses are read", meaning the there is
little time to understand and fully appreciate roses, and by
extension, the meaningful and beautiful things in life.

Kings that rule over "subjects in dread" themselves
become the subjects of flowers that they end up provid-
ing fertilizer for after their death. The reader is admon-
ished to enjoy the ephemeral beauty of life and nature
before it is too late. Why it will be too late if one does not
make the most of time is the subject of the surprise ending in the last line. One expects it to read something like
"Brief is the time that they will be red." But this would not
be a good argument, since there will always be more roses
to replace them. The final line shocks the reader by directly
reminding him or her of his or her own mortality, which
logically follows from the thesis of the poem: if everything is
ephemeral, the reader cannot be an exception.

I like the following couplet a great deal:

"Like fire, love, and water, the white of the moon,
Streaked sunsets in amber, the call of the loon."

Note that, in addition to the statement these lines make, they illustrate the fact that originally fresh and interesting rhyming is not only a function of the words rhymed, but also of the words around them. "Moon" with almost any word is considered trite, if the reader only considers the words that are rhymed.

This poem is an example the multidimensional poetry I advocate in the introduction. In addition to the main theme, it has a subtle, underlying theme of the interrelatedness of all phenomena: butterflies taste flowers, referring to the ecological interdependence of plants and insects; dead people fertilize roses; the white of the moon of line 10 comes from the sun of the sunsets of line 11. The beauty of nature is another underlying theme.

The first seven lines of the poem rhyme with each other by ending with the phonetic sound, "ed", then the next six are couplets without this sound, and then the poem finishes with a couplet with the "ed" sound again; and no rhyming word is ever used a second time. And the last "ed" rhyme word, which is also the last word of the poem, is the shocking "dead". The words at the end of all of the "ed" rhyming lines, including the end couplet, listed in order, are: "red, bled, shed, head, dread, instead, fed, bed, dead". Interestingly, all seem to go together in a common theme, at least to a point, many conjuring up images of blood and death.

Speaking of red roses has the ring of a cliché; it has been used a good deal in poetry and song before. Here it is used with a simple rhyme scheme. All this is deceptive, strengthening the poem by partially hiding the deeper meanings of the poem discussed in the previous paragraphs. It adds a subtlety to the poem and makes it interesting by hiding deeper meanings in what appears to be a greeting card type of verse. There is a history of the use of the rose in poetry, and this poem draws on that to a small extent; for example, one is reminded of Robert Herrick's poem, *To the Virgins, To Make Much of Time*, which starts "Gather your rosebuds while ye may", and has the theme of the brevity of life and how little time we have to enjoy it.

The one time the word "brief" is substituted for a new word is in line 3, where "short" replaces it and allows an alliteration with "shed" at the end of the line, strengthening the theme of the ephemeral nature of the precious things of life, through sound.

the only enduring reality

This poem is somewhat obscure, not lending itself to easy comprehension, but the basic meaning, that pain is the only enduring reality, is spelled out in the last four words. The most interesting aspect of this poem is that the words "tears", "wind", and "wound" each have two pronunciations, with each pronunciation having a different meaning than the other, and "course" has a double meaning (is a pun). Both of the two meanings of each of these four words are workable in reading and interpreting the poem. Since all *combinations* of the meanings of these four words represent acceptable interpretations of the poem, the poem can be read in sixteen different ways, each with a unique meaning, and all sixteen interpretations are valid and make sense. There are a total of eight different pronunciations in the sixteen different ways to read the poem.

So Human a Predator

I wrote two versions of this poem, one much longer than the other. The reasons for this are explained immediately above the two versions of the poem.

For both the longer and shorter versions of the poem

Without overtly stating it, this poem makes an analogy between people and the caged black panther: Just as the panther does not understand his cage's bars, and hence does not see that it is going nowhere and pacing in vain, so people, in this poem and in general, go nowhere, pursuing impossible goals and repeating maladaptive, often painful behaviors that fail to bring results, often for their entire lives, without knowing it or understanding why.

For the longer version of the poem only

The poem has interesting, lively, original use of language ("lassoing the wind"), and effective references to cats, leopards, and black panthers when discussing the people ("lion hopeless"; "ignored in black leopard sugar"). Some interesting line breaks give added meaning to lines.

Note that a panther is a melanistic (black) leopard, which occurs only in the Old World, in this poem. Some leopards are born black; these are called panthers. This is not to be confused with the puma or mountain lion of North and South America, which is sometimes called a panther; this cat is known by many other names as well. In addition, the jaguar, also ranging in North and South America, has a black form sometimes referred to as a panther. I use the adjective "black" to modify panther in stanza 1 of both versions of the poem to be certain that the reader does not think I am talking about a mountain lion; otherwise, this word would not have been included. Stanza 3 of the longer version refers to a panther in an Old World forest, eliminating the possibility of a mountain lion or a melanistic jaguar as the subject of the poem, leaving no possibility other than the melanistic leopard as the black panther of this poem.

Human and Mole

Think about this poem. By the poetic device of comparing and contrasting humans and moles, it is commenting on a condition common to many people.

Green to Green

Lines 2 through 5 each have something that is green or associated with the word "green" changing to something else that is green or associated with the word, always going from a better to a worse state. The poem appears to be commanding the reader to make these changes happen, but in fact this is a poetic device: the poem is describing what actually happens in the real world.

Dead Alive

The effective last line shocks and brings the poem's thesis into focus succinctly and pointedly.

Lament

Notice the metaphors and poetic phrases. I would not be doing you a service to point out specific instances of these; it is best you exercise your brain and find them yourself, assuming you have not already done so.

Seasons

Each stanza discusses a different season, as a metaphor for a human life. In stanza 3, lines 3 through 5 make puns with words with multiple meanings. It is worth thinking about the poetic language and meaning of line 1 of the last stanza. By the way, I like that line a great deal.

Awe and Wonder

Notice the imagery and poetic language. I intended that they would evoke awe and wonder, re-enforcing the suggestion that the poem presents.

Black

Of course, black symbolizes the unknown, the mystery. Repetition of the word "black", and references to things that are either the color black or in some way related to uncertainty, re-enforce the idea that it is best to accept, even embrace and love, uncertainty (since there will always be a large part of reality that is not known to us, and questions that we cannot fully answer with certainty).

Notice the difference in meaning between line 1,

"Black, God how I want you black,"

and line 10,

"Black God, how I want you black."

Sky Wisdom

I believe that science has profound philosophical implications, and is even probably the best source to use as the basis or foundation for some philosophical questions. It is a good, perhaps the best, way to throw light on and work toward understanding many of the big questions that concern us, such as how we got here, our relationship to the Universe, and where we are headed. This poem expresses that belief.

I donated this poem to the Chabot Space and Science Center, in Oakland, California, which is appropriate, because this museum is an astronomy and space science museum with telescopes for the general public to view the skies. They accepted it, but did not have it on display at the time of publication of this book, although they may sometime in the future. They are keeping it in their archives.

The reason the last stanza is set apart by a dashed line, and why I do not consider that stanza to really be part of this poem, is explained above the poem.

Winds of August

Rhyming couplets and rhythm go with the theme of the poem.

Let me make a few comments about stanza 3. Lines 5 and 6 of this stanza say:

> "Wafting pagan tales and creeds
> Into Christian myths and deeds."

The word "myth" has two definitions relevant here. A myth is a fictitious story. It is also a traditional story, which is not necessarily fictitious, serving to explain some phenomenon of nature, the origin of humans, or the customs, institutions, religious rites, etc., of a people. Since the second definition of myth could apply to this line, it does not necessarily say Christian stories are fictitious. A deed is any act, so can include (and here does include) the use of symbols, such as the Christmas tree and mistletoe; rituals; and celebrating holidays like Christmas. The lines refer to the fact that many Christian stories, ideas, holidays, and symbols were taken and modified from paganism. Examples include Christmas, the Christmas tree, and Easter.

As far as some lines later in the stanza are concerned, the speaker of the poem is not anti-Christian, but argues that Christian values have been lost.

Nature's Nature

Personifications of the wind as wailing, the sky as crying tears of rain have been used enough in poetry to be clichés. But here the last stanza reveals that the wind and sky are *not* personified, in a novel twist with a surprise ending that shows the theme of the poem to be the indifference and unconsciousness of nature. The poem points out that the metaphors of the wind wailing and rain crying to people wailing and crying is limited to the sounds made and falling of water, and does not apply to the conscious sorrow people feel, for the wind and rain do not experience this.

Alliteration re-enforces the poem's meaning and theme.

Line 2 of stanza 3 is correct in stating that the lily

"fades before the fade of day,"

because there are species of lily that fade the same day that they bloom.

I've Known Oceans

In stanza 1, line 3 is not literal, since the sea's waves do not ebb and flow in synchrony with our pulse; it refers to the deep connection we have to nature, and hence the connection all things have to each other. The sea water that leaked into our arteries (line 5) refers to our evolution. No (or know) God is used in three different senses in a powerfully philosophical play on words in line 8.

Stanza 2, line 14 says,

> "controlling me as currents direct plankton,"

and has a play on words on "current", which can refer to the electrical current carrying messages along neurons in the brain, as well as ocean currents.

There is a great deal of delightful poetic language and other interesting things that you should discover on your own.

Each stanza ends with an interesting, profound pun.

No It U Love

The title of this poem, "No It U Love", is evolution spelled backward.

In stanza 1, line 1, and in some subsequent stanzas, is, "Edit DNA, Emit". This is "time and tide" spelled backward. Hence, in lines 1 and 2 of this stanza,

> "Edit DNA, Emit—wait,
> for no man",

is equivalent to: "Time and tide wait for no man," except for differences in punctuation. Variations of this "wait for no man" phrase also appear as a refrain at the start of stanzas 3 and 6, and as the two closing lines of the poem.

In stanza 1, line 8, "MOM and DAD" is "DAD DNA MOM" spelled backward. Line 9 points out that MOM upside down is WOW.

171

A palindrome is a word, phrase, or sentence that is the same spelled backward and forward. The many palindromes, and spelling of phrases backward to create other meaningful phrases, in this poem, are consistent with and re-enforce the poem's thematic question of whether the Universe is a palindrome.

Following is a list of all the palindromes in the poem, listed under the stanza number, with the line number listed in front of each one. In this list, l. stands for line number; e.g., l. 1 means line number 1.

Stanza 1:

l. 8:	MOM
l. 8:	DAD
l. 16:	name no one man

Stanza 2:

l. 7:	love? And time, Emit? DNA evol

Stanza 3:

l. 3:	dog, cod, doc, god

Stanza 4:

l. 1:	Was it a rat I saw?
l. 2:	oozy rat in a sanitary zoo
l. 5:	rats live on no evil star
l. 7:	emit time
l. 15:	evolvers rev love
l. 20:	rats lived on no devil star
l. 21:	no devil lived on
l. 22:	devil never even lived!
l. 23:	Do geese see God?

Stanza 5:

l. 1:	Sums are not set as a test on Erasmus
l. 7:	I prefer pi

Stanza 6:

l. 2:	not a ton
l. 5:	dumb mud
l. 6:	add A
l. 7:	can I attain a C?
l. 9:	and E. T. saw waste DNA?
l. 10:	Edit peptide
l. 10:	DNA land
l. 12:	bar crab
l. 14:	no garden, one dragon
l. 15:	tuna, nut
l. 15:	bird rib
l. 17:	camel in Nile, Mac
l. 18:	dog, elk, cat, emu, ("me tackle God...")
l. 20:	stack cats
l. 22:	I tip away a wapiti
l. 24:	God, wasp saw a dog
l. 25:	gnat sums mustang
l. 27:	may a banana nab a yam
l. 28:	Swap paws
l. 29:	late fetal
l. 33:	go, do, dog
l. 34:	step on no pets
l. 36:	God! Nate bit a Tibetan dog!
l. 39:	lion, O, puma, I am upon oil!
l. 40:	deer gas? I disagreed

Stanza 7:

l. 1:	On a Toyota? No!

Stanza 8:

l. 1:	Egad, a base life defiles a bad age
l. 2:	doom an evil deed, liven a mood
l. 3:	live not on evil, Madam, live not on evil
l. 9:	Now I won
l. 10:	no evil I did, I live on
l. 12:	no evil shahs live on

There are several puns, plays on words, intentionally mis-spelled words that yield double meanings, and line breaks that go with these. Take, for example, stanza 1, lines 11 through 13:

> "the two as-
> specks of light, part-
> tickle and wave,".

Another example is stanza 4, lines 8 to 13:

> "pre-ordained pat-
> terns fly over wholly sea
> of Uni-
> verse be-
> fore play
> of life results."

Also, line 14 of this stanza points out that the word "evolve" has the word "love" in it spelled backward, and puns on this when it states, "Evolve holds love in a backward spell,".

There is the example of stanza 8, lines 4 to 6:

> "that your life will have harmony, not
> harm on Y, nor X, chromo-
> some. Some,…"

Line 11 of this stanza has a play on words resembling the word "palindrome": "…pal, in dramatic…".

Finally, lines 1 and 2 of stanza 5 state:

> "Sums are not set as a test on Erasmus,
> neither Desiderius nor Darwin's granddad;".

Desiderius Erasmus of Rotterdam (1466/1469-1536) was a Dutch Renaissance humanist and Catholic Christian theo-logian. Erasmus Darwin (1731-1802) was the grandfather of Charles Darwin, and had an early theory of evolution of his own that largely anticipated most of what his grandson would later propose, except for the important idea of natu-ral selection.

The Origin of Species

To write this poem, I took the last paragraph of Charles Darwin's book that presents his theory of evolution by natural selection, *The Origin of Species* (published in 1859). I added my own line breaks, changed some of the wording and punctuation a small amount, and changed some capitalized words to lower case, to make it into a poem.

The last paragraph of Darwin's scientific masterpiece is a beautiful combination of poetic prose and science. Enjoy the beautiful language as well as the scientific statement, although the latter is not by any means a comprehensive summary of evolution by natural selection. I hope you also enjoy my line breaks and other minor alterations.

If you want to see Darwin's original paragraph from which I wrote this poem, his *Origin of Species* was first published in 1859. Later editions of it have been published by several publishing companies, and many booksellers and libraries carry it.

Death

Line 32 states: "We play the bugle with the fife;". The bugle is used to awaken soldiers in the morning, so here it symbolizes dawn, awakening, beginning, new life, birth. In the song entitled "The Streets of Laredo", the dying cowboy commands, "Play the fife...", so here this instrument symbolizes death.

Fingers of Nightshade

The nightshade is a deadly, poisonous plant. So, "fingers of nightshade hide in the blue", which summarizes much of the poem's theme, means the terrible specter of death is always hiding as an awful reminder. Thus, there is a double meaning, with nightshade also meaning shades of night. The poem as a whole is saying that death is always hiding and lurking in the deeply beautiful, wonderful experience that life is.

In "deserts of night loom in bloom", the word "loom" is in the word "bloom". So "loom in bloom" is a play on words.

The line, "flight of the Kite", has "Kite" capitalized to show that I am referring to the bird, not something people fly on a string. If this were used in prose,, one would use lower case because this does not refer to a specific species of kite, which would be capitalized; for example, the White-tailed Kite.

The line "I love the cat that walks under the June" is not a line that can be explained verbally, but is to be understood with the right brain and intuition, and appreciated for what it evokes.

Consider the lines:

> "reflections on earth as it is in seven
> stars of the Pleiades."

It sounds like reflections on earth as it is in Heaven. The Pleiades, also called the Seven Sisters, is a beautiful cluster of stars in the constellation Taurus.

In the last stanza, there is a play on words: "sweet tea" symbolizes the sweet flavor of the drink of life, and "t" is the first letter of "true", while "rue" is the sadness that life must end and the last three letters of "true".

Explore the alliteration, assonance, effects of line breaks, and especially word play and puns, as well as other poetic devices in other lines on your own, especially the following lines:

> "hide in the blue even,
> even as awed as
> intelligent life in
> the Universe is

a merry-go-round turned by
beauty and love
are its music"

"All we touch takes
the spirit of gold
within, without
the curse of King Midas"

"the nightshade
can fade,
hide in the glade, or even
the green that leaves the trees,
and even as much of the green lives on
its fingers are
a phantom for rest for the rest of the forest"

"empty stomach biting zero"

"a starling in starlight,
Saturn's silver
(silver rings shiver,
deliver a sliver of white in the slight)"

last psalm

Line breaks make interesting lines that have their own
separate meanings that are whole phrases or thoughts, interestingly supplementing and re-enforcing the poem as a
whole. Examples of this are "in a man-" and "cloud crow-"
and "wren's screams" and "motion, wheel".

There are puns on both words in "wheel dye". A good
interpretation of this line is that the speaker finds it too terrible
to express these two words in the other spelling of "we'll die".

Unclear raw is an anagram for nuclear war, and this
poem is about how the human race will die in a nuclear war
with tremendous irony: the destruction of all higher life on
earth caused by humans will be terribly beautiful and visible
to people as the human race and all higher life forms die off.

Duende

Duende is a Spanish word and is a characteristic of any art—painting, sculpture, song, dance, and so on—that the Spanish look for as something that deeply moves them and makes the work great, but is not solely competence—it is a quality that suggests death and/or the dark side of life. See the work that inspired this poem for more information on duende: *Theory and Function of the Duende*, a lecture delivered by the Spanish poet, Federico Garcia Lorca, in Havana, Cuba, and Buenos Aires, Argentina, translated by J. L. Gill, who also supplied notes; this work can be found in *Poetics of the New American Poetry*. It is probably published other places as well. Notice the imagery in this poem.

Note that the audience gave the same response (silence) to the singer's two performances, even though their internal reactions to her performances were very different.

Marriage in the Key of Ebony and Ivory

This poem celebrates the fact that rock and roll music is a fusion of Black rhythm and blues (henceforth, r & b) and White country and western (henceforth, c & w) music. It is full of word plays, puns, and anagrams, most of which refer to rock and roll songs or artists.

In stanza 3, lines 7 through 9, is a pun that does not refer to any such songs or artists:

"They sang, though, like coyotes that howl at the moon,
    Of life in a prison or in a saloon;
It made some folks wonder, between the blue bars:".

These lines have a pun on "bars" with three meanings. The bars of their singing, bars of the prisons they sang of life in, and bars that were the saloons they sang of life in. Also, these lines with line 10 of this stanza express a thought similar to the idea expressed in a stanza in the traditional cowboy song, "Home on the Range".

Stanza 4, line 3, states,

"Up on Haley's Comet, some claim came the start".

This refers to the fact that many people credit the first rock and roll record to a band called Bill Haley and the Comets ("Rock Around the Clock").

In stanza 5, line 2, there is also a pun that does not refer to any song or artist:

"This time to Great Britain to set a new score."

Here, "score" can mean to score a victory or points, something being set up ("set a score"), or a musical score. Following is a list of most of the puns, word plays, and anagrams that do refer to songs of rock and roll or popular music that is a precursor of or related to it, and/or the artists of these musical pieces, in the poem, listed under the stanza number, with the line number listed in front of each one. In this list, l. stands for line number; e. g., l. 1 means line number 1.

Stanza 2:

l. 2: "On the platters of Doo Wop": A platter can refer to a record, and the Platters were a Doo Wop group that was among the first to fuse r & b with c & w in the early days of rock and roll.

l. 4: "only the lonely": the name of a hit song by the rock and roll artist, Roy Orbison.

Stanza 3:

l. 2: "home on the range": the name of an old traditional c & w song.

Stanza 4:

l. 4: "Holly was planted" is a pun on holly the plant and '50's rock star Buddy Holly; "Oh Boy!" was the name of one of his hits, yielding a pun on the song's name.

l. 5-6: "Good Golly, Miss Molly" was a song by Little Richard; a direct thrill is an anagram for Little Richard. His music was more on the r & b side of rock, as opposed to the c & w side. The popularity of an African American musician like

Little Richard with White teenagers, and their dancing to his music, upset some of their parents, especially since his music was considered wild at the time.

l. 7-10: "Eve yells, rips" is an anagram for Elvis Presley, noted for being able to sing both the White c & w and Black r & b with great skill. "All Shook Up" was an early hit by Elvis Presley.

l. 11-12: "King...coal...gnat": Nat King Cole.

l. 14: "couldn't chuck, bury, or vanquish...": Chuck Berry, rock and roll musician.

l. 15: "Black in the country": Chuck Berry, a Black man who was excellent at the r & b side of rock and roll, was also a master of the c & w side of rock, not only in his singing and playing guitar, but in his composing of songs.

l. 17: "He hot; cay ebbs" is an anagram for The Beach Boys, a surf music band. This group's leader was Brian Wilson, who wrote most of their songs and sang in a high falsetto. "Cay ebbs high" is a pun: a sandy cay is a low island that could be near good surfing areas, and the (musical) key ("cay" is pronounced "key") ebbs high because of Brian Wilson's falsetto. (To really make sense, the island meaning of the pun requires "tide" and a word or two as words that are understood: "cay ebbs at high tide", or "cay is high at ebb tide". It does not make a lot of sense to say a "cay ebbs high", when one is using "cay" to refer to an island). Wilson's falsetto also accounts for the end of the line, "falsetto's his turf".

l. 18: Chuck Berry influenced Brian Wilson's music composition. Wilson used the tune of Berry's hit "Sweet Little Sixteen" when he wrote the Beach Boys' hit "Surfin' USA".

l. 19-22: African American women sang a good deal of the hits that the brilliant rock and roll record producer, Phil Spector, a White man, produced in the sound he created called the "wall of sound". One such singer was Darlene Love. Another group of Black women who Spector produced records for was the Crystals.

l. 23: Surf music groups tended to be White.

l. 24-28: Chuck Berry "won" (that is, won over, influenced) Brian Wilson, referred to as "smile-brain" because he is the composer and main musician of the important album, *Smile*. "Won smile-brain" is an anagram for "me, Brian Wilson". Although Brian Wilson was arguably the leading composer and was certainly a major recorder of surf music with his band, the Beach Boys, he never surfed, hence the phrase "who never rode boards". There is a pun here for the surfing purists, who object to a composer of surf music who never surfed in his life: And *bury one* smile-brain (who never rode boards). "With the help of sweet voices, and fill up once more": This pun means "...and fill up your cups and drink to the sweet music one more time", but also means "with the help of...Phillup (Phil Spector) once more". "Be My Baby" was a hit that Phil Spector produced by a group consisting of Black women called the Ronettes. You've *been it* before is a pun in that the lead singer of the Ronettes was Veronica *Bennett*. The pun also sort of works in a historical sense in that Veronica Bennett was Phil Spector's wife for a while (during which time she was known as Ronnie Spector). (By the way, the Ronettes got their name from Veronica, known as Ronnie, Bennett). "Be My Baby" was a favorite record of Brian Wilson's, and influenced his Beach Boy hit, "Don't Worry, Baby". "Black guides surf again" is a play on words in that it sounds like "Black rides surf again".

Stanza 5:

l. 3-8: The pun on Buddy Holly is repeated from earlier in the verse, but the pun on Chuck Berry is a wholly different pun than previously used on his last name (this time, it's "berry", the fruit; previously, "bury", the verb, was used). "Waters of mud" refers to Muddy Waters, Black blues musician, who, like Buddy Holly and Chuck Berry, influenced the Rolling Stones. "So sing rotten Hell" is an anagram for the Rolling Stones, a band of White musicians who mastered

181

the r & b side of rock, including blues, and had the hits "(I Can't Get No) Satisfaction" and "Brown Sugar").

l. 9-10: "Clapped on" is a play on words for (Eric) Clapton, another White who mastered r & b and blues. A great guitarist, he played with the groups Cream, Blind Faith, and the Yard Birds. He was in the Yardbirds before he was in the other two groups. Since the Yardbirds' music was innovative, and since Clapton (and other musicians in that band) moved on to new innovations in subsequent bands, the Yardbirds did not "sit still".

l. 11-14: "There's a Place" and "Eight Days a Week" are hits by the Beatles, arguably the best rock and roll band ever, and Whites who mastered both the c & w and r & b (again, including the blues) facets that united to form rock and roll. "The best ale" is an anagram for the Beatles.

When I credited a group or musician with mastering either r & b or c & w, I did not mean to imply the group or musician did not master the other.

Stanza 6 argues that nothing is more important than bringing two races together, and that the fusion of the music of the White and Black races was and is the best way to bring about fusion and harmony between the races. This makes the fusion of r & b and c & w and the birth of rock and roll a symbol of something much more comprehensive and significant, taking the poem to a new level of meaning.

The last line of the poem is identical to the first line, except the order of the words "Black and White" are reversed to "White and Black", while preserving the ab rhyme scheme, tying up the theme of the fusion of Black r & b with White c & w to make the beautiful music called rock and roll.

I donated this poem to the Stax Museum of American Soul Music, located in Memphis, Tennessee. They accepted it, but did not have it on display at the time of publication of this book, although they may sometime in the future. They are keeping it in their archives.

I Dream of Ebony

This poem is about race envy, and has an extraordinarily unusual and radical thesis in that the speaker is a Caucasian envying those of the African race, seeing them as in touch with their emotions, and himself as out of contact with his. Since society generally views the Caucasian race as privileged and the African race as oppressed, the poem has a brave, radical thesis.

I hope that the unthinking politically correct will not misconstrue this poem as disrespectful to African Americans. This is not intended. A careful reading of the poem reveals that it is obviously not disrespectful, and nothing in the poem would support such an idea, but I include this paragraph because of the danger for misinterpretation that happens too often in today's world.

The poem's first two lines have a pun:

> "Race envy,
> and you'll always lose."

Lines 6 and 7 of stanza 1 have a line break that makes line 6 alone have a different meaning than when it is read with the first word of line 7:

> "bursting, so it is
> said".

Lines 4 to 6 of stanza 2 have plays on words on "white" and "white out":

> "bleaches emotion
> white out
> of existence".

Lines 9 and 10 of this stanza have a meaning-altering line break that is also a pun:

> "just loco-
> motion".

Stanza 3, lines 5 and 6, present an interesting near-rhyming, philosophical couplet:

"The leaves that feed the branches
are the ones that do the dances".

In this stanza, line 9 has a deep two-word pun on whether/weather and morning/mourning, giving a combination of four possible meanings, but with the pun on morning/mourning being more powerful and making more sense. Here it is with lines 8, 10, and 11, to give context:

"Only the oppressed know
whether morning
dew is the tears of night
or sweat of a new day."

Also in this stanza, lines 12 and 13 speak of feeling the isolation of an albino crow. Besides the reference to being of the White race, there is biological truth here: An albino crow feels isolated because animals that are radically different from others of their own species tend to be shunned by them.

Lines 6 through 9 in stanza 4 are of interest because Harlem is referred to as a bower and Soweto as a garden, which is quite ironic and different than they are usually thought of.

A similar ironical twist is found in the first four lines of stanza 5, but the irony is reversed, speaking of the "deserts of White", "prisons of Beverly Hills", "and "little mansions".

This stanza has interesting alliteration and word play in line 5: "white wanes to wan". It also uses the word "bars" as a noun and a verb in a pun in line 13:

"My blank heart on the other side of
my brain-dungeon bars
my emotion,".

And this stanza has a play on words appropriate to the mental state of the speaker in line 16: "Luna, ticking".

Pieces of April

There is an interesting line break between the first two lines of stanza 2:

> "I have fragments of sun-
> Rise at the end of the day."

Taken together, the lines have one meaning. They have a very different meaning than when taken separately as a result of this line break:

> "I have fragments of sun-"
> and
> "Rise at the end of the day;".

In stanza 4, line 1, "cadmium moon dreams" is a nice, interesting phrase.

Lines 3 and 4 of the final stanza present an interesting metaphor of our past as a dragon that we cannot slay.

There is a pun on morning/mourning in the poem's last line.

Y Knot

Obviously, the lamb is Jesus Christ, and the poem draws from Christian theology and the well-known song we all learn as children, "Mary Had A Little Lamb". The title has many plays on words and meanings. Why not save Himself? Why did the lamb's crucifiers tie Him in a knot after all the good He had done? He should not have a Y chromosome because only males have Y chromosomes, not females, yet He was born of a virgin birth. From a purely scientific, biological point of view, females can give birth to offspring without males, but in such cases, only females can be born (Y not; that is, not Y). Of course, I know the objections to this reasoning from a non-scientific, religious point of view, and I realize this could be considered carrying an argument to a silly extreme, but this is just a fun play on words, not to be taken as a serious argument.

The philosophical point that this poem raises is something the reader can spend some time contemplating to great profit. In general, when and why should one NOT save oneself (that is, sacrifice oneself) for the sake of others? The question of why Jesus did not save Himself can and perhaps should be contemplated, although some would say this has already been answered. The point is that the question can be generalized and need not be limited to Christ.

Jesus, How You've Changed!

Notice and enjoy the puns and plays on words, especially the ones with Biblical references and references to stories about Christ. For example, in stanza 2, we have:

> "One good fry day,
> the Christ-shams cooked all your love
> out of you,
> set you on across
> a river of blood and
> hate,..."

Contemplate stanza 6: Christ and His teachings are good and should be known by the fruit they bear, but (some of) the fruit (His pseudo-followers who twisted His teachings) is poisoned. Thus, one cannot know Him by that fruit. It is only when the fruit is poisoned that the wisdom, "By their fruit you will know them", fails to hold true.

Interesting line breaks cause the meaning of individual lines to differ from the lines taken together as a whole, as in the beginning of stanza 9:

> "They have you advocating sex
> education is not to be permitted in schools;
> no birth
> control permitted
> of any kind,..."

The end of the poem makes reference to, even borrows from, the famous poem, "The Second Coming", by William Butler Yates, in an interesting way.

This poem is not anti-Christian or meant to be offensive to Christians. Rather, it is an indictment of those who twisted Christ's teachings from those of love to those of hate. And yes, as far as one claim of this poem and the previous one is concerned, the Bible clearly supports the idea that Jesus fought against empire–the Roman Empire.

Red

Could the speculation that the fate of the blood of our race is strawberry jam refer to the human race eventually being figuratively squished to a red-colored jam by going extinct in a nuclear war, ecological catastrophe, or natural disaster, such as a huge meteor crashing into the earth? What about the double meaning of jam, with the possibility of the human race getting into a strawberry jam?

To Restrict Freedom

The poem is in the shape of a flag, which is related to and re-enforces its meaning, because the flag is often considered a symbol of freedom.

The pattern of adding a syllable, a word, or a letter to the previous line and keeping the rest of that line is easy to see, and sticks to a few consistent rules.

Individual lines have their own meanings, which are often interesting, and which help build the poem's theme and add tension. Sometimes a line even contradicts a previous line.

The poem has a surprise ending.

Rhythm Method

No comments.

The Greatest Hits of Neptoon Rising

Look up any definitions that you need to in this poem in the punabridged dictionary.

Sleepwalk or Something

This poem is meant to be humorous and frivolous. The puns and plays on words regarding subjects such as the Holy See, the Swami, the Sikh, and so on are playful and not meant to be offensive. I realize that they obviously are not offensive in this playful context, especially since the poem does not say or imply anything bad about the subjects in question, but I am meticulous about disclaimers when issues of this nature might arise.

Poem Without End

None, which is zero, which is a number that is circular.

ALPHABETIZED INDEX OF THE POEMS

This section consists of two columns. The first column lists the page number of the poem itself, while the second column lists the page number of the author's commentary on the poem.

ALPHABETIZED INDEX OF FIRST LINES OF THE POEMS